"This book is a rare treat—a fireside chat with a battle-tested Christian CEO who has led big organizations in both the secular and ministry worlds. Rich Stearns offers a master's-level course on leadership with faith as his north star. Embrace these seventeen leadership values and you will become a better leader and a better ambassador for Christ."

John C. Maxwell, author of *The 21 Irrefutable Laws of Leadership*

"Steady. Reliable. Focused. These are the words I use to describe Richard Stearns. I've known him for two decades, traveled with him to distant lands, and partnered with him in multiple projects. He leads with impeccable integrity and skill. I'm thrilled to read this book and gladly commend Rich to you as the perfect person to write it."

Max Lucado, pastor and author

"Rich Stearns has written a book that we have all needed as leaders for so long, one that lifts the importance of values over success by human standards. Living faithfully is much harder than producing results that make us look smarter than we really are. This book will challenge your character and remind you of what really matters to God."

David Anderson, author of *Gracism*, pastor of Bridgeway Community Church

"Richard Stearns is a leader not only to admire because of his successes but also to learn from because of his honest self-reflection about his failures. Interwoven as these two necessarily are, Stearns lays them out before us here with humility, candor, grief, faith, and hope. Thank you, Rich Stearns, for leading like it matters to God. It shows."

Mark Labberton, president, Fuller Theological Seminary

"My friend Rich Stearns is a leader who is humble and unafraid, a rare combination. He knows that justice and mercy are not incompatible and that we all are called to speak both truth and love. I have had the privilege of watching Rich lead with the courage and humility needed for difficult times like this."

Bill Haslam, former governor of Tennessee

"In a time of crisis when the very values that make up 'Christian' leadership seem to be woefully rare, Rich Stearns is one of the voices that I most need to speak into my own life and leadership. Stearns opens his heart and shares his own experience in the struggle of becoming—and remaining—a leader who demonstrates the values of what matters most to God. I will return to this book again and again."

Tod Bolsinger, Fuller Seminary, author of *Canoeing the Mountains*

"Sit down and read Rich Stearns. It's like a privileged conversation with a wise mentor who really cares about you. Aristotle wrote that *why* is the most important question. In a world full of *how* books, Rich answers why Christian leadership matters."

Leith Anderson, president emeritus of the National Association of Evangelicals

"As we are facing racial injustice, gender inequality, and extreme global poverty, among other issues, this book challenges us to believe that surrendering our ideas of success to God can lead to not only inner transformation but world-changing impact. The church needs to rise up to meet these challenges by pointing to a better way rooted in truthfulness and love, and this book is the right tool at the right time to help us on that journey."

Jenny Yang, vice president for advocacy and policy, World Relief

"In *Lead Like It Matters to God* you will find brilliant answers. Rich doesn't provide five new methods for brilliant hiring or seven ways to personal motivation. Instead, his brilliant book is about something almost forgotten in our seminaries, leadership seminars, and even in our pulpits—Christian *virtues*."

Ray Johnston, lead senior pastor, Bayside Church

"What struck me right between the eyes was that there are hundreds of 'how-to' books on leadership, but I can't think of one 'why-to' book, which to me is the essence of true leadership. Rich has written the book that needed to be written, and there is no one more qualified to write it."

Ron Blue, author of *Master Your Money*

"Some leadership characteristics like surrender, courage, and perseverance you can only teach if you have lived them out for many years, or your teaching will ring hollow. Having watched Rich lead for over twenty years, I not only admire his integrity, but I have witnessed him surrendering his own agenda, digging down deep for courage in very tough times, and persevering to make the kind of leveraged eternal impact that we all desire."

Lloyd Reeb, founding partner of the Halftime Institute

"The book *Lead Like it Matters to God* is a much-needed text for leaders and aspiring leaders who see themselves as kingdom ambassadors in the marketplace. Richard Stearns eloquently describes how a believer's ultimate mission is to know, love, and serve God in whatever environment or position one finds him- or herself. This book is both timely and needed for such a time as this."

John K. Jenkins Sr., senior pastor, First Baptist Church of Glenarden, Maryland

"*Lead Like It Matters to God* is a leadership book like no other. This entire book weaves Rich Stearns's experiences from many years of leading in the secular business world and the Christian global nonprofit world with lessons learned, principles to practice, questions to ponder, and examples of both success and failure. A book for these times! A book for now and future leaders who will join God in changing the world for good."

Jo Anne Lyon, general superintendent emerita, The Wesleyan Church

"There are, it has been said, two sets of virtues or values. The *résumé virtues* relate to a job well done, and the rewards are more external—recognition, success, popularity, achievement, material benefits. The *eulogy virtues* signify a life well lived, and the rewards are more internal—a sense of purpose fulfilled, of benefits to others, of spiritual well-being. Rich Stearns in his remarkable career has experienced and valued both sets, which is why this honest and personal reflection on leadership is so important. In an age that values what is seen and temporal, Rich Stearns points us to what is unseen and eternal."

Leighton Ford, Leighton Ford Ministries

"For years, I have hoped that Rich Stearns would write this very book. Here he guides us through the lessons he has learned along the way. This book will equip and inspire you as you lead, in whatever place God has put you, by enabling you to listen to a battle-tested leader who has earned our trust."

Russell Moore, president, the Ethics & Religious Liberty Commission

"Whether you are a first-time leader or an experienced leader, the challenge of leadership is ever present and ubiquitous. Rich Stearns's years of leadership experience and acumen help leaders at all levels calibrate their foundation of leadership that is values-based and internal, before moving to the external. Engaging with this book will not just help you increase your leadership influence—it will help you become the leader God created you to be!"

Tom DeVries, CEO of the Global Leadership Network

"Rich Stearns is extremely transparent as he shares his lifelong experiences. I appreciate how each chapter carries a refreshing dose of humility. His desire to know, love, and serve God reminds us that a life surrendered to Christ is missional in *every way* and in *every assignment*. This book is a gift to all leaders, wherever you are in your transformational journey."

Tami Heim, president and CEO of Christian Leadership Alliance

"*Lead Like It Matters to God* isn't just about leadership but also about discipleship. In other words, while it will clearly speak to leaders, it will also resonate with anyone who desires to grow as a follower of Christ. In a culture that often obsesses about success at all costs, Richard Stearns has given both the church and the larger culture an important and timely resource."

Eugene Cho, president, Bread for the World, author of *Thou Shalt Not Be a Jerk*

"We reap the benefits of Rich Stearns's decades of rich, high-level leadership experience in these pages. His insights and reflection on his own career framed through the lens of Scripture challenge readers to flip the script of what the world considers success and to reframe leadership uniquely as a follower of Christ."

Gary Haugen, founder of International Justice Mission

"Rich reminds us that God's metrics for leading have more to do with faithfulness and fruitfulness than the twin temptations of success and pride. Servant-leaders from churches to government will be challenged and inspired. It's an idea whose time has come!"

Gabriel Salguero, president of the National Latino Evangelical Coalition

"I was a raving fan of Rich Stearns while he was president of World Vision US. Now I know why, after reading his book *Lead Like It Matters to God*. I learned, as Rich did, that even though I fall short of perfection, if I trust God, I still can learn to lead like it matters to him. If you read this book, I know that will happen to you too. Then watch the careers and lives of the people around you soar."

Ken Blanchard, coauthor of *The One Minute Manager* and *Servant Leadership in Action*

"In writing about values-centered leadership, Rich offers a compelling vision of what Christ-centered, kingdom-valued leadership can look like. I have observed and experienced firsthand the humble, thoughtful, and effective leadership of Rich Stearns. It is an honor to give my highest endorsement for a leadership book that presents important content offered from the narrative of a leader with great integrity."

Soong-Chan Rah, Robert Munger Professor of Evangelism at Fuller Theological Seminary

"Richard Stearns has written a remarkably helpful book that lays out the key *biblical* values of leadership faithfulness. *Lead Like It Matters to God* is a treasure trove of wisdom from a seasoned leader who has sought to model biblical fidelity in the businesses and organizations he has led. Enjoy learning leadership not from a theoretician but a practitioner."

Ed Stetzer, Wheaton College

"It is refreshing to read a leadership book that keeps God's kingdom in focus and is grounded in biblical principles. Richard Stearns has written a practical resource for godly people who want to lead by their values."

Natasha Sistrunk Robinson, author of *A Sojourner's Truth* and *Mentor for Life*

"This leadership book is unusual because the author uses some of his own setbacks and failures to teach essential leadership virtues. Many leadership authors only share the glossy side of winning at leadership. Yet we often learn most from our mistakes. In *Lead Like It Matters to God*, Rich Stearns turns the world's version of leadership upside down to posit that who you are is more important that what you achieve."

Shirley Hoogstra, president, Council for Christian Colleges and Universities

"Grounded in Scripture and real-world experiences, Rich Stearns helps us reflect on who we're becoming and exhorts us toward values-driven leadership. A much-needed book in this season when we're longing for leaders with character, and a must-read for any Christian leader!"

Tom Lin, president/CEO of InterVarsity Christian Fellowship

RICHARD STEARNS

LEAD
LIKE IT
MATTERS
TO
GOD

**VALUES-DRIVEN LEADERSHIP
IN A SUCCESS-DRIVEN WORLD**

17 VALUES TO TRANSFORM YOUR LEADERSHIP

An imprint of InterVarsity Press
Downers Grove, Illinois

InterVarsity Press
P.O. Box 1400, Downers Grove, IL 60515-1426
ivpress.com
email@ivpress.com

InterVarsity Press® is the book-publishing division of InterVarsity Christian Fellowship/USA®, a movement of students and faculty active on campus at hundreds of universities, colleges, and schools of nursing in the United States of America, and a member movement of the International Fellowship of Evangelical Students. For information about local and regional activities, visit intervarsity.org.

All Scripture quotations, unless otherwise indicated, are taken from The Holy Bible, New International Version®, NIV®. Copyright © 1973, 1978, 1984, 2011 by Biblica, Inc.™ Used by permission of Zondervan. All rights reserved worldwide. www.zondervan.com. The "NIV" and "New International Version" are trademarks registered in the United States Patent and Trademark Office by Biblica, Inc.™

While any stories in this book are true, some names and identifying information may have been changed to protect the privacy of individuals.

The publisher cannot verify the accuracy or functionality of website URLs used in this book beyond the date of publication.

Cover design and image composite: David Fassett
Interior design: Jeanna Wiggins
Image: compass illustration: © Sigit Mulyo Utomo / iStock / Getty Images Plus

ISBN 978-0-8308-4730-3 (print)
ISBN 978-0-8308-4731-0 (digital)

Printed in the United States of America ♾

InterVarsity Press is committed to ecological stewardship and to the conservation of natural resources in all our operations. This book was printed using sustainably sourced paper.

Library of Congress Cataloging-in-Publication Data
A catalog record for this book is available from the Library of Congress.

P	25	24	23	22	21	20	19	18	17	16	15	14	13	12	11	10	9	8	7	6	5	4	3	2	1
Y	42	41	40	39	38	37	36	35	34	33	32	31	30	29	28	27	26	25	24	23	22	21			

THIS BOOK IS DEDICATED, WITH GRATITUDE,

to the hundreds of colleagues, mentors, teachers,

and friends whose character and leadership shaped,

changed, and inspired me over the course of my career.

Values lived out can become infectious—in a good way.

So I am especially grateful to those "contagious"

colleagues, who by their own examples showed

me how to become a better leader—

a leader more pleasing to God.

But seek first his kingdom and his righteousness,
and all these things will be given to you as well.

MATTHEW 6:33

But the fruit of the Spirit is love, joy, peace,
forbearance, kindness, goodness, faithfulness, gentleness
and self-control. Against such things there is no law.

GALATIANS 5:22-23

CONTENTS

INTRODUCTION

The aim of life is not to gain a place in the sun, nor to achieve fame or success, but to lose ourselves in the glory of God.

SAINT IGNATIUS OF LOYOLA

LET ME START WITH A CONFESSION: I don't generally enjoy reading leadership books. I think that's because they always make me feel a little inadequate—like I don't quite measure up because I haven't mastered the latest leadership methods and techniques. So it's kind of ironic that I have now written a leadership book. Heaven knows there are literally hundreds of books out there, each hawking some approach that will lead to greater success, some new formula that will transform and catapult our careers. And I don't object to any books that will help leaders become better at leading because leadership matters a great deal in our world. Good leaders can change the world in remarkable ways—just as bad leaders can do serious harm.

But as a Christian, I have come to believe that God's design for leadership is radically different from the secular models that so dominate the current landscape and have seeped into churches and ministries as well. Secular models are almost always outcomes based.

1

They focus on what skillsets, what techniques, what leadership behaviors will deliver superior results. Good results and better performance are not bad things, but in God's economy, they are not the main thing. In a world where success is king, we must be careful not to fall into the trap of believing that our identity somehow derives from the magnitude of our achievements rather than our relationship with God. I believe God is far more concerned about how a leader leads than he is about the success that leader delivers. Because success is overrated.

Yes, you heard me correctly, I said that success is overrated. Now I understand that making this statement, in a book about leadership, is akin to heresy. We live in a success-obsessed culture where winning is everything—in business, in sports, in politics, in school, and in life. We celebrate the wealthiest people, the most powerful leaders, the biggest churches, the winningest teams, the fastest-growing companies, and the most famous celebrities. We are literally marinating in a success-driven, achievement-oriented culture that permeates every dimension of our work and our lives. The drive for success and achievement is so pervasive that we don't even realize how much it influences everything that we do. It's like a colorless, odorless gas that we are all breathing. But it can be deadly. The dogged pursuit of success can become an idol in our lives that lures us farther and farther away from God. But God, as it turns out, is not all that interested in success. He is not impressed by growing revenues, increased church attendance, the size of your income, or the title on your business card. God is looking for leaders "after his own heart," winsome leaders who will submit to his leading and trust him for the outcomes. A leader's character matters more to God.

Right now, you might be thinking: Easy for you to say. You don't know what I face every day at work. It's perform or perish. I work in a dog-eat-dog environment. It's a brutal workplace culture. If you don't perform, you're out, and you might be out even when you do perform if you get on the wrong side of the workplace politics. On Sunday at church I hear about "putting on the full armor of God," but on Monday, if I want to make it through the week, I need to put on the full armor of the world. Because work sometimes feels like combat.

If that's what you're facing in your job, I totally understand because I worked in just those kind of tough, secular environments for almost twenty-five years. I have had some horrible bosses, worked in some toxic cultures, and have even been fired twice. But through all of it I learned that my Christian faith was not a liability, it was an asset. In the midst of all the stress and pressure, I discovered that when we truly take God with us to work, he will use us for his purposes.

WHEN WE TRULY TAKE GOD WITH US TO WORK, HE WILL USE US FOR HIS PURPOSES.

Mother Teresa, who was sainted by the Catholic Church for her lifelong dedication to the poor in India, once made a profound statement that thoroughly shatters our secular notions of success. Senator Mark Hatfield was visiting her in Calcutta and watching as she moved among the beds of the sick and dying. The senator was struck by the sheer size of the needs compared to the resources she had available. "Mother," he asked, "don't you get awfully discouraged when you see the magnitude of the poverty and realize how little you can really do?" In a respectful way he was really asking her if she felt like she was failing in the face of those overwhelming odds. She answered him with this: "My dear

Senator, God did not call me to be successful. He called me to be faithful." Wow! In just fourteen words Mother Teresa flipped our "success paradigm" upside down—God calls us to be faithful, not successful.

You see, we tend to put the highest value on the outcomes of our work, but God values our motives more. We value the "what" of our work, but God values the "why" and the "how." We prioritize the destination, but for God it's all about the journey. We reward success, but God's bottom line is faithfulness. This single truth flies in the face of most of what we've been taught about leadership in books, seminars, universities and our workplaces.

I don't know about you, but I sometimes imagine what it will be like someday to stand before the Lord and to hear his assessment of

WE REWARD SUCCESS, BUT GOD'S BOTTOM LINE IS FAITHFULNESS.

my life. And despite my three CEO titles and decades of working in multiple organizations, I just can't imagine God saying to me: "Well done, good and faithful servant, for those twenty consecutive quarters of earnings growth!" or, "Way to go, Rich, on becoming a CEO at the age of thirty-three. You killed it!" No, I don't think God will be impressed by those things. Hey, my wife isn't even impressed by those things. It's far more likely that God will speak to us about *how* we led and *how* we lived. How did we represent him to those we worked with? How did we embody the truths and values of the kingdom of God in our lives? And how did we tangibly show his great love for people in our daily conduct?

For most of my twenty years as president of World Vision, I had 2 Corinthians 5:20 stenciled on my office wall: "We are therefore Christ's ambassadors, as though God were making his appeal through us." This verse, more than any other, seemed to capture my role as a Christian leader. Jesus was calling me to be his ambassador. And ambassadors are called to embody the values, ideals, and character of the one they represent. I will make the case in these pages that wherever you work or volunteer—in a school, a business, a church, a ministry, a nonprofit, in government, or in your home—you too are called first to be Christ's ambassador. God really is making his appeal through you. It's a humbling thought, isn't it? It doesn't matter whether you consider yourself a leader or not. You're Christ's ambassador. Your life *is* your witness whether you are at work or at home. When people look at how you live your life, raise your children, spend your money, do your work, and treat others, what will they see? These things matter most to God.

This book is about why I believe the values Christian leaders embrace are more important than the success they achieve. I am not arguing that success is a bad thing—it's just not the main thing. Character and competence are both honoring to God. When we focus first on being faithful to God in our lives, and when our work is driven by the values of God's kingdom, he may very well bless us with successful outcomes. But qualities like integrity, humility, excellence, perseverance, generosity, courage, and forgiveness matter more to God than the most impressive résumé of accomplishments. And I believe that leaders who embrace these characteristics will lift not only their own performance but also the performance of their teams.

However, as I'm writing this book, these timeless Christian values are under assault in our culture. Corporate scandals happen with regularity. Cheating scandals have again been uncovered in professional sports. The #MeToo movement has revealed appalling abuses of power by men toward women in virtually every sector of our society: corporate America, Hollywood, the media, academia, government, and even within the church. The coronavirus epidemic has tested leaders in every sphere and shown us the values on which their leadership is based—some to their credit and others to their shame. Tragically, blatant racism and xenophobia have again reared their ugly heads in our country with incidents of police brutality exposing deeply systemic racial biases. And our national politics have devolved into the basest kind of lying, name calling, and incivility in my lifetime. What has happened to our values?

This book is about reclaiming those values.

The beauty of becoming a values-driven leader is that embracing positive values does not require you to master any exceptional new skills or techniques. Values-driven leadership is more about character than capabilities, more about being than doing, more about pleasing God than people. So, I have organized the book around seventeen values and leadership qualities that I believe are essential for a Christian leader to embody: surrender, sacrifice, trust, love, excellence, humility, integrity, vision, courage, generosity, perseverance, forgiveness, self-awareness, balance, humor, encouragement, and listening. After a couple of introductory chapters, each of these values is expanded on in a chapter of its own, supported by Scripture and illustrated with stories from my own experiences. You can read them sequentially or you can jump to one of the values that seems most relevant to you right now.

Now it takes a fair bit of hubris to think one is qualified to write a book about leadership. So I need to begin with a heartfelt confession. I was never a perfect leader—not anywhere close. Over the course of my career my warts and blemishes were on display for everyone to see. As a leader I have made serious mistakes, failed many times, handled situations badly, and disappointed God more often than I'd like to admit. But throughout it all I tried to pick myself up, dust myself off, and try again to become a better leader— a better ambassador for Jesus. My hope for this book is that younger leaders might benefit from the important life lessons of a fellow traveler—someone who now has the great advantage of hindsight. You can chalk these insights up to experience or you can see them as accumulated wisdom, but my sincere hope is that you will find them helpful.

I wrote this book because I believe leadership is so very important. Leadership affects every dimension of our human experience. Leadership can unite us, lift us up, and inspire us to achieve great things. And leadership is crucial to accomplishing God's purposes in our world. In short, leadership matters to God and so it ought to matter to us.

LEADERSHIP CHANGES THE WORLD

JOINING THE REVOLUTION

SCRIPTURE ➤ "We are therefore Christ's ambassadors, as though God were making his appeal through us." (2 Corinthians 5:20)

LEADERSHIP PRINCIPLE ➤ Christian leaders are called to be change agents for Christ, bringing healing and restoration into the brokenness of their communities and workplaces.

Let every man abide in the calling wherein he is called, and his work will be as sacred as the work of the ministry. It is not what a man does that determines whether his work is sacred or secular, it is why he does it.

A. W. TOZER

Never doubt that a small group of thoughtful, committed citizens can change the world; indeed, it's the only thing that ever has.

MARGARET MEAD

Margaret mead, the famous anthropologist, was right. When you stop and think about it, virtually every accomplishment of the human race over the millennia has been achieved not by single individuals, but by the collective effort of groups of people who have joined together in some sort of organized way. When groups of people come together, each contributing different skills and abilities, the whole is always much greater than the sum of the parts: one plus one plus one can equal fifty.

Let me give you just a few examples. Do you ever marvel at everyday miracles like skyscrapers, automobiles, smartphones, vaccines, suspension bridges, or even the flat-screen TV in your home? None were achieved by a single person. They were the result of the collective efforts of large groups of people working together, often standing on the shoulders of other groups of people that came before them. The people who built your TV had to rely on the past achievements of those who learned how to produce glass, refine steel and aluminum, injection-mold plastics, broadcast radio signals, and create semiconductor circuits. In fact, your television is the product of thousands of groups of people working over thousands of years adding one innovation after another to the total of human knowledge.

So, what's my point? Groups of people working together change the world. And groups of people always need to be led. Without leadership, groups of people are just, well, groups of people. Without leadership, they might as well be herds of cows. Why does one sports team win the trophy over all the others? Leadership. Why does one company outperform others? Leadership. Why does one church committee accomplish more than others? Leadership. It is not an exaggeration to say that all human achievements have been made possible by leaders who provided direction and vision to groups of people, enabling the groups to accomplish something that none of the individuals could have achieved alone. Leadership is the one critical ingredient that changes the world.

But there is a myth about leadership that I would like to debunk. We tend to put leaders on pedestals. We glorify them in our culture as some sort of super race of beings. But in reality leaders are just one cog in the machinery of human endeavor, one member of the team. Of what use is a symphony conductor without her musicians? What good is a coach without his players? What is the value of the committee chair without her committee? There is an important symbiosis between the leader and the led. In 1 Corinthians 12, the

LEADERSHIP IS THE ONE CRITICAL INGREDIENT THAT CHANGES THE WORLD.

apostle Paul described the church using the metaphor of the interdependencies within the human body. It is a wonderful picture of the importance of every member of a group, not just the leader.

> Even so the body is not made up of one part but of many. . . .
>
> But in fact God has placed the parts in the body, every one of them, just as he wanted them to be. If they were all one part, where would the body be? As it is, there are many parts, but one body.
>
> The eye cannot say to the hand, "I don't need you!" And the head cannot say to the feet, "I don't need you!" On the contrary, those parts of the body that seem to be weaker are indispensable, and the parts that we think are less honorable we treat with special honor. And the parts that are unpresentable are treated with special modesty, while our presentable parts need no special treatment. But God has put the body together, giving greater honor to the parts that lacked it, *so that there should be no division in the body, but that its parts should have equal concern for each other.* If one part suffers, every part suffers with it; if one part is honored, every part rejoices with it. (1 Corinthians 12:14, 18-26)

Essentially Paul was saying that the body only functions because all its parts are different, and each plays a critical role. No one part of the body, not even the head, can function without the others. Steve Jobs could never have brought us the iPhone without a legion of designers, engineers, marketers, accountants, and programmers behind him. Abraham Lincoln could never have freed the slaves and preserved the union without brave social activists, other voices in Congress, his own cabinet members, and the Union Army.

For the Christian leader, there is another truth in this passage that should be the bedrock of his or her leadership philosophy: "there should be no division in the body," and "its parts should have equal concern for each other." Every member of the group you are leading is precious, deserves honor, and is uniquely gifted by God. People want to follow a leader who values them in that way.

And, while I'm at it, there is another leadership myth that needs debunking. Leaders are not rare. Almost all of us are leaders. The CEO, the symphony conductor, or the school principal are not the only leaders in their respective institutions. In my CEO roles I had multiple vice presidents reporting to me who were also leaders. And they had directors and managers reporting to them who were leaders. The school principal has department chairs, coaches, librarians, and so on—each of whom is a leader in their own sphere. The conductor has the heads of each instrumental section. Most organizations have many leadership roles. The truth is that most of us are both followers and leaders at the same time, being a member of one team and the leader of another. And even if you have a job with few leadership duties, you may be a leader at your church, in your neighborhood, or in your family.

THE "WHY" OF LEADERSHIP

So why does leadership really matter to God? You're probably reading this book because you want to become a better leader in your chosen profession. You work hard and you hope to get recognition, promotions, expanded responsibilities, and, yes, more money. Those things are the "what" things. They may be things you are hoping to achieve, but they don't answer the "why" questions. Why do you do what you do? Why is your work important to God? The "why" questions start to get at things like purpose and meaning, which require us to think much more deeply about our lives in Christ.

For most of us, there doesn't seem to be much of a connection between the God we worship on Sunday and the work we do on Monday. I spent twenty-three years of my life working at companies that sold deodorants, toys and games, and luxury tableware (Gillette, Parker Brothers Games, and Lenox China). But did God really care about my work in those places? And did my work really matter in God's larger purposes in the world? The answer is a resounding yes, but perhaps for reasons that are not immediately obvious. To understand how our work connects to our faith, we need to go back into our Bibles to discern just what God wants to accomplish in the world and why we, those of us who are followers of Jesus, play such a crucial role in the unfolding of God's plan. There is a big picture here that we need to see if we are ever to understand how our lives— and what we do with them—matter to God. To put it in business terms, our personal mission or calling needs to flow out of the mission of God in our world. So, bear with me as I unpack a little theology. Because without understanding the theological underpinnings of our vocations, the work we do for forty or fifty hours a week for maybe forty years won't integrate very well with our faith.

13

GOD IS CALLING US TO JOIN HIM
IN CHANGING THE WORLD

Fundamental to my understanding of the mission of every follower of Jesus Christ in our world is this statement: I believe that Jesus came to launch a revolution that would fundamentally change the world in profound ways. A revolution he called the coming of the kingdom of God.

JESUS CAME TO LAUNCH A REVOLUTION THAT WOULD FUNDAMENTALLY CHANGE THE WORLD IN PROFOUND WAYS.

If you were to read through the four Gospels looking for the words "kingdom of God" or "kingdom of heaven," you would conclude that Jesus was totally preoccupied with the *coming* of such a kingdom. This "kingdom coming" idea is mentioned more than a hundred times in the Gospels, mostly by Jesus himself. To take this even a step further, after a fresh reading of the Gospels using this "kingdom" lens, you would likely conclude that the central mission of Jesus' incarnation was to purposefully inaugurate and establish God's kingdom on earth.

So just what was this coming of the kingdom of God all about? It was essentially Jesus' world-changing vision of a new relationship between God and humankind—a relationship that could now begin to heal the brokenness of the human race and renew God's creation, conforming it to the character and likeness of God. It was his vision of a new way of living, a new dream for human society that would turn the values of the world inside out as people chose to live under God's rule and according to his values. And he intended it to change the world.

In the introduction to this book I quoted 2 Corinthians 5:20, the verse I had stenciled on my office wall, which calls us to be Christ's ambassadors. But let's now look at that verse in context.

> Therefore, if anyone is in Christ, the new creation has come: The old has gone, the new is here! All this is from God, who *reconciled* us to himself through Christ and gave us the *ministry of reconciliation*: that God was *reconciling* the world to himself in Christ, not counting people's sins against them. And he has committed to us the *message of reconciliation*. We are therefore Christ's ambassadors, as though God were making his appeal through us. We implore you on Christ's behalf: Be *reconciled* to God. God made him who had no sin to be sin for us, so that in him we might become the righteousness of God. (2 Corinthians 5:17-21)

There is a lot in this passage we could unpack, but let me draw your attention to the word *reconcile/reconciliation,* used five times in these verses. In the Greek, the word for reconciliation is *katallagē,* which means "restoration to (divine) favor." Merriam-Webster defines *reconcile* this way: "To restore to friendship or harmony; to make consistent or congruous." In other words, this "ministry of reconciliation" is about restoring people to friendship and harmony with God and making all things more consistent and congruous with God's desires.

On a personal level this reconciliation occurs through the forgiveness of our sins through Christ's atonement, which restores us to a right relationship with God. But on a grander scale, this ministry of reconciliation also extends out into our world. Christ's followers, now forgiven and restored, seek to restore all things to favor with God: individuals, families, communities, schools, businesses, organizations, governments, and nations. God has commissioned us as his ambassadors to be involved with his grand renewal and restoration project in a broken and fallen world. As followers of Christ, we are invited and directed to participate in his great redemptive rescue mission.

In the Lord's Prayer we find a remarkable statement that we often just recite by rote: "Thy kingdom come, thy will be done, *on earth as it is in heaven.*" The coming of the kingdom of God is not just about some heavenly future; it is very much intended to play out right here on earth. As Jesus' followers, we are sent into the world to begin the process of reconciling all things to God. This is Jesus' vision of his transformed disciples transforming the world.

WE ARE INVITED AND DIRECTED TO PARTICIPATE IN CHRIST'S GREAT REDEMPTIVE RESCUE MISSION.

We personally join Jesus' kingdom revolution by *repudiating* the values of this world—greed, arrogance, selfishness, hatred, racism, sexism, domination, exploitation, and corruption—and *modeling* the values of God's kingdom: love, justice, forgiveness, integrity, sacrifice, encouragement, generosity, humility, inclusion, and compassion. We are called to become ambassadors for and purveyors of these kingdom values, which work to restore the brokenness of humanity. "Therefore, if anyone is in Christ, the new creation has come: The old has gone, the new is here!" (2 Corinthians 5:17).

FIREFIGHTERS OF THE KINGDOM

To take this out of theological terminology, one way I have described this kingdom mission is compare it to the way our white blood cells function in our body. (My long-ago degree in neurobiology has given me just enough knowledge to be dangerous.) Essentially, when our body experiences brokenness because of a wound or infection, our white blood cells rush to the site of the brokenness to repair, restore, and heal. Or, to use another metaphor, our white blood cells are the body's "firefighters," rushing to put out fires. I think this is a beautiful picture of the role of the church in our broken world. We are called to circulate in every part of our world and our cultures to bring healing and restoration wherever we find brokenness. And human brokenness is found everywhere—in families, communities, schools, businesses, and governments.

As followers of Jesus Christ, who first healed our brokenness, all of us are now called to be his ambassadors, serving as his agents of healing and restoration wherever we live and work. This is the "why" of our lives and work. This is our core mission and purpose wherever God may have placed us. This is why our work matters to God. The British theologian N. T. Wright puts it this way:

> Our task as image-bearing, God-loving, Christ-shaped, Spirit-filled Christians, following Christ and shaping our world, is to announce redemption to a world that has discovered its fallenness, to announce healing to a world that has discovered its brokenness, to proclaim love and trust to a world that knows only exploitation, fear and suspicion. . . . The gospel of Jesus points us and indeed urges us to be at the leading edge of the whole culture, articulating in story and music and art and philosophy and education and poetry and politics and theology and even—heaven help us—Biblical studies, a worldview that will mount the historically-rooted Christian challenge to both modernity and postmodernity, leading the way . . . with joy and humor and gentleness and good judgment and true wisdom. I believe if we face the question, "if not now, then when?" if we are grasped by this vision, we may also hear the question, "if not us, then who?" And if the gospel of Jesus is not the key to this task, then what is?

LEADERSHIP FOR WHAT?

You signed up to read a book on leadership, but the past few pages of theology may have seemed like a bit of a bait and switch. But it is only when you understand that you are engaged in a revolution to change the world for Christ that the true purpose of your leadership role becomes real. God's agenda of reform and redemption, as his kingdom comes "on earth as it is in heaven," targets every human institution. Leaders shape communities, corporations, schools, hospitals, charities, and governments. Christian leaders can shape them to conform more to the heart of Christ, who loves the people who work there.

I asked earlier whether God really cared about my work at Lenox, Parker Brothers, or Gillette. The answer is yes. Work is inherently valuable as we use our unique talents and abilities in ways that reflect God's own creativity to produce products and services that benefit the broader community. Work also provides needed livelihoods for individuals and families. But, perhaps more significantly, our workplaces matter because they are human institutions filled with people whom God cares about. God wants all people to flourish and to be drawn into relationship with him. And so, if God's kingdom is to expand and grow, every human institution must also be renewed by the values and principles of his kingdom revolution. Organizational cultures can be brutal, or they can be life-giving. Good and godly leadership contributes to human flourishing when it creates cultures and environments that are fair, just, and caring.

GODLY LEADERSHIP CONTRIBUTES TO HUMAN FLOURISHING WHEN IT CREATES CULTURES AND ENVIRONMENTS THAT ARE FAIR, JUST, AND CARING.

CALLED TO MAKE A DIFFERENCE

A few months after I left my CEO job at Lenox China to join World Vision, I called my former executive assistant, Maureen, to see how things were going back at Lenox. I was troubled to hear her report. She said something like this, "Rich, it's just not the same here now. The atmosphere is so negative. It seems like everyone is out for themselves. Even the language is coarser. People are hurting here now." Then she said, "Can you come back?" Now, after years of working together, I know that Maureen was biased, but what she was saying was that leadership matters—it makes a difference. To be honest, during my years at Lenox I wondered more than once whether my Christian faith made any difference at all. I had a Bible on my desk and tried to treat people in ways that were humane and caring, but I didn't always feel like I was making a difference for the Lord. But at some level I was shaping the culture and values of Lenox to be more pleasing to God. Christian leaders shape and influence institutions, and that matters. Integrity, excellence, humility, forgiveness, encouragement, trust, and courage are values of the kingdom of God. And when leaders incarnate those values, the world changes. God had placed me on the front lines of his revolution at a place that happened to sell fine china and crystal. Lenox mattered to God, and the place where you work matters to God too.

2

THE PLANS I HAVE FOR YOU

A BIT OF AUTOBIOGRAPHY

SCRIPTURE ➤ "'For I know the plans I have for you,' declares the LORD, 'plans to prosper you and not to harm you, plans to give you hope and a future.'" (Jeremiah 29:11)

LEADERSHIP PRINCIPLE ➤ God has been present in your life since before you drew your first breath. He wants to use all your talents, abilities, and life experiences to shape you and prepare you to serve his purposes. God is calling you into his great purpose for your life.

If you believe in a God who controls the big things,
you have to believe in a God who controls the little things.
It is we, of course, to whom things look "little" or "big."

ELISABETH ELLIOT

Hindsight is so much clearer than foresight.
As I look back on my life and career, I can see more clearly the many

ways God shaped my character and directed my steps that were barely perceptible at the time. And here's what I've learned about God's leading: while he always leads us in the direction of his intended purpose for our lives, he also lets us decide whether we will follow. The ball is in our court. And, "following" doesn't just involve the big decisions made at life's great crossroads moments. It requires a daily submission, a consistent obedience in life's small moments. Follow him in the small things and he may someday use you to achieve great things. You are God's hands and feet in this world, and he will use you if you'll let him.

FOLLOW GOD IN THE SMALL THINGS AND HE MAY SOMEDAY USE YOU TO ACHIEVE GREAT THINGS.

WE ALL START SOMEWHERE

I was born and raised in Syracuse, New York. My father was a used-car salesman with an eighth-grade education and my mother a filing clerk who never finished high school. When I was born, my father optimistically ordered a new neon sign to display over his small used-car lot reading: "Ed Stearns & Son—Used Cars." Like most fathers, he hoped that someday his son might become successful, even though success always seemed to elude him. My dad was kind of a tragic figure—a man with little education and an alcoholic with three failed marriages. His drinking problem not only ruined his marriages but also caused him to fail in business. Ultimately things fell apart, creating a downward spiral that caused our family to unravel. My father loved us, but he just wasn't able to cope with the pressures of life. When he was finally forced to declare bankruptcy, my mother left him, and the bank foreclosed on our home. At ten years old, my family and my world unraveled.

Over the next few years my mother, sister, and I had to fend for ourselves, struggling financially and moving from one rental house to the next until I finished high school. Of course, the ordeal of these childhood events shaped me in various ways. On the one hand, I was forced to become more self-reliant, but on the other, it instilled in me a deep sense of insecurity that I carried well into my adult years.

But despite the turbulence in my life, I lived in an America where all things seemed possible, and I grew up at a time when the right education could open the doors to the world. I now realize that I also grew up at a time when just being a white male opened opportunities for me that were effectively closed to women and minorities. The American dream was not fully available to everyone, nor is it still today.

As a young boy my dream was to escape from the things that had killed the dreams of my parents and to find a better and different life on the other side. And while my difficult childhood might have held me back, it actually had the opposite effect; it motivated me to work hard to avoid the mistakes my parents had made. My older sister, Karen, instilled in me the notion that education could offer both of us a pathway out. So, at some point in my early teens, I set my hopes on the possibility that I might someday attend one of the Ivy League universities, which my sister assured me were the very best places to go. But in order to pursue this, I knew I would need something my family didn't have—money. So, I worked a succession of summer and part-time jobs: delivering newspapers, bagging groceries, selling popcorn at a movie theater, and even cleaning toilets at a nursing home. But it was those early jobs that taught me the basics about work, money, and responsibility. And toward my college dreams, I tried to save almost every penny I earned, not fully appreciating that all my years of savings would barely pay for my first semester of tuition.

ANYTHING'S POSSIBLE

There were eight Ivy League schools, and one, Cornell University in Ithaca, New York, was just fifty miles from my home in Syracuse. Since I had never traveled to another state, Cornell was about as big a dream as I dared to have. And so, when the time came, it was the only college I applied to. When I told my mother I wanted to go to Cornell, she actually laughed. "And just who's going to pay for that? Not me, and certainly not your drunken father!" I replied that I wasn't sure how, but I would find a way.

And I did. With youthful naiveté, I worked hard on the application, sent it in, and was accepted. To my amazement, I was offered several critical scholarships that brought my dream within reach. My first semester at Cornell felt like shock treatment. Given my family and educational background, I discovered that I was totally unprepared to compete academically with sons and daughters who had come from more supportive families and gone to better schools. That first year I studied furiously, knowing that, unlike most of the other kids there, I was performing without a safety net, so failure was not an option. thats when GOD takes over, (when theres no PLAN B)

Cornell provided me with much more than just an education—it was a crucible that taught me how to think, reason, and survive under pressure; it was a doorway to a new world of possibilities. Four years later, I graduated with a BS in neurobiology and animal behavior—a degree that was relatively worthless unless one wanted to become a doctor or a professor, which I did not. I loved the sciences, but neurobiology had been a bad choice for someone piling up a mountain of student loans and who would need to find a job upon graduation. During my senior year, feeling mounting pressure to find gainful employment, I decided to apply to business schools to get an MBA, reasoning that just about everything was a business of some sort. And a business degree would get me a job. I applied to four schools and got accepted into three of them. But the fourth school was the prize—the school I dreamed of attending—the Wharton School at the University of Pennsylvania. It was always listed as one of the top two or three business schools in the country, and it was another one of those Ivy League universities.

So I was crushed when I didn't get in. Instead, the school put me on a waiting list. At least I hadn't been rejected. I still had a chance. Wharton was truly the school of American dreams—a school whose degree could "punch your ticket" to success. So, I decided to call the admissions office to see whether I could talk my way in. I explained how very much I wanted—no, needed—to get into their program, but to no avail. I got their standard spiel: "We have our process and we will review the waiting list in May after we see how many spots are available." Undeterred, I called again the next week and once more explained how badly I wanted to go there. Same response. And I called again the next week and the next and the next. I called every week until the May deadline. I wanted this. And then, finally, a letter came in the mail. I had not only been accepted but had been given a substantial scholarship! To this day I don't know if my nagging persistence made the difference, but I have to believe it helped. That summer, to earn more money, I drove a taxi in Syracuse, shuttling business types to and from the airport. My aspiration was that in just a few years, for the very first time, I might be able to ride in the back seat of a taxi.

I arrived at Wharton that September wearing cut-off shorts and sandals with hair down to my shoulders. I didn't even own a suit and tie. When I tried to attend the first new-student orientation, I was actually stopped at the door by a security guard because I didn't "look like an MBA student." I had to show them my ID to get in. Now inside the auditorium, I could see that most of my fellow classmates were five to ten years older and were wearing suits and carrying briefcases. So, after sitting through the orientation, I went straight to the campus barber. "Can you make me look like a Wharton MBA student?" I asked. He flashed me a big smile and said, "I would love to!" And then he sheared me like a sheep.

GOD CALLING

But I need to back up a few months. Something else of great significance happened to me toward the end of my senior year at Cornell: I met my future wife, Reneé, on a blind date—a date that was to change my life forever. In a previous book I have told this story, but it bears repeating here. I was a senior and Reneé a freshman. I was just a month from graduating and so didn't expect much to happen on a blind date so close to leaving Cornell. And Reneé was what we called a "Jesus freak" back then, complete with her Campus Crusade for Christ evangelism training. We were an odd pairing. After four years at Cornell, I was pretty much an atheist who believed that God was for weak people who needed crutches, and I didn't need a crutch. So, our encounter that night was a clash of worldviews. We were so different that it was hard to find things to talk about. But at some point during the evening there was a lapse in our conversation and Reneé reached into her purse and pulled out *The Four Spiritual Laws*. I don't know about today, but back then every "Crusader" had been trained to use it as an evangelism tool. It led a person through the steps required to become a Christian, and at the end it asked for a commitment.

I was actually a bit amused when she asked if she could share this with me. "Really? You're really going to do this?" Reneé responded that she was quite serious and asked if she could continue. I agreed and sat there as she dutifully explained the Christian faith to me. She started by telling me that God loved me and had a wonderful plan for my life. I was skeptical, listening impatiently as she went through the booklet, already thinking about my rebuttal. But there was one page that really jumped out at me toward the end. It showed two small diagrams of a chair or "throne" and asked the question: "Who is on the throne of your life?" One diagram showed a throne with "self" on it, surrounded by chaos and disorder. The other showed Christ on the throne, producing a coherent and ordered life. The point was that for me to become a follower of Jesus Christ, I would have to allow him to be in control of my life, and I would have to surrender. My reaction was visceral: "No way!" I had gotten through my childhood and college years by taking control of my own life and not trusting it to anyone else, and I wasn't about to start now. So, I told Reneé that while all of this was interesting, maybe it wasn't for me. But some small voice within me was urging me to reconsider, to listen to what she had said. We ended up having a great conversation about life and faith and our hopes and dreams for the future, and I realized there was something about this young woman that I was drawn to. A spark had ignited between us. And for the next month before my graduation we saw each other almost every day.

That summer, decades before email and texting, we wrote letters every day, with her in California and me back in Syracuse driving my taxi. The relationship seemed to be getting more and more serious. But the following November, during my first semester at Wharton, Reneé made the difficult decision to break off

(Don't be Afraid to ask the Question)

our relationship, finally accepting that I had no interest in her Christian faith. She knew she could never marry someone who didn't share her deepest beliefs. It was hard for both of us but courageous of her to stand on her beliefs no matter the cost.

My parents had not been religious. They were culturally Catholic but never attended church. Being divorced back then usually meant you were not welcome in the church. And so I had no religious role models growing up. My years of self-reliance had convinced me that religion was for the weak, and after four years in the sciences at Cornell, I was going to do it "my way," as Frank Sinatra had so famously crooned.

But Reneé's decision devastated me and set me off on a quest to learn more about this Jesus who had caused me to lose the love of my life. There was much to learn, so I began reading and studying and asking every question about Jesus and the Christian faith I could think of. Months later, after reading more than fifty books on Christian apologetics, philosophy, and comparative religion, I came back to that question—who is on the throne of my life? More importantly, who did I want to be on the throne of my life? And that very moment I knew. I understood that surrender was the only way to faith, and that faith in Jesus Christ was the only way to life in all its fullness. Through my reading I became convinced that Jesus really was who he said he was, the Son of the living God. And so, on that very day in my dorm at the Wharton School, after finishing one final book, *Miracles*, by C. S. Lewis, I surrendered. I said, "Not my will but thy will," and I promised that I would now live with Jesus on the

I UNDERSTOOD THAT SURRENDER WAS THE ONLY WAY TO FAITH, AND THAT FAITH IN JESUS CHRIST WAS THE ONLY WAY TO LIFE IN ALL ITS FULLNESS.

throne of my life. I mumbled some words about doing what he called me to do, going where he called me to go, and being who he wanted me to be. Little did I know the plans he had for me. That one decision changed the entire trajectory of my life.

ADVANCE TOKEN TO BOARDWALK

And now I'll go quickly. Yes, Reneé and I got back together and were married sixteen months later, just after our graduations. And Wharton did "punch my ticket." In the middle of a recession, I got four job offers and signed on with the Gillette Company in Boston, where my first job was to help promote underarm deodorant, foot deodorant, and shaving cream. (You've got to start somewhere.) And I did get to ride in the back seats of taxis with some regularity. While I started working at Gillette, Reneé went off to law school at Boston College and became an attorney providing legal services to the poor.

After two years of peddling shaving cream and deodorant, I left Gillette for a better job with Parker Brothers Games in Salem, Massachusetts. And I loved my new job. I was being paid to play games like Monopoly, Clue, Sorry, and Risk! Parker Brothers had also invented the Nerf ball and in the early 1980s made an entry into the emerging video games market. I spent the next nine years there. Advancement opportunities came quickly. It seemed like I was at the right place at the right time just about every time. About seven years in, and thoroughly unprepared for the role, I was promoted to president and CEO, at the tender age of thirty-three. Reneé took to calling me "business boy."

This was what I had dreamed of. I had made it. I had finally succeeded in overcoming the challenges of my family background. I naively expected that I would spend my whole career at Parker Brothers but would soon learn that God had other plans for me beyond games and Nerf balls. During those years. Reneé and I started our family, and the first three of our five children were born.

INTO THE WILDERNESS

It seemed like everything in our life was going well during those years—until it wasn't. After less than two years as president, I was abruptly fired when the company changed ownership. Losing a job is always hard, but for me this felt especially traumatic. In an instant, everything I had worked for was gone, and I found myself struggling with my old childhood anxieties over failure and insecurity. Instead of taking adequate time to reflect with the Lord, I threw myself into a job search and took the first offer that came my way. I was hired four months later by the Franklin Mint, the mail-order collectibles company, and we moved our growing family from Massachusetts to Pennsylvania. But just nine months later, I was fired again. The second time was even harder. But this time I spent long hours with the Lord, praying and reading Scripture. God was obviously trying to get my attention, and he used this time "in the wilderness" in powerful ways. More on this later.

After nine more months of prayer, reflection, and job searching, I was finally offered a position at Lenox, the grand old maker of American fine china and crystal. I must say that leading a fine china tableware company was not my childhood dream, but nevertheless I was thrilled to be back to work. They hired me to be the president of their smallest division, which had been losing money for several years, but it was a foot in the door at a great company. So, I accepted and dug into my new position with gratefulness to God.

Things worked out very well for me at Lenox as I grew professionally, met lots of new people, and got my career back on track, this time with a greater sense of how my faith integrated with my work. I spent the next eleven years at Lenox, eventually being promoted all the way to CEO. I was finally back on top and grateful to God for this new season in my life.

THE PLANS I HAVE FOR YOU

Once again, I thought I would spend the rest of my working career at Lenox. But God . . . yes, God had other plans for our lives. Those plans presented themselves one day when an executive recruiter called me informing me that the Christian ministry World Vision was looking for a new CEO. Apparently, I had the perfect résumé: neurobiology, deodorant, board games, collectibles, fine china, and crystal. Yes, I was the ideal candidate for a role that involved helping the poorest children on the planet. But that phone call ended up changing our lives. God was inviting me to trade my success for something much more significant, but I would have to let go of my version of the American dream. God was again asking me to surrender to his will for my life, and that surrender did not come easily. But he had been preparing me for that moment for years.

With great apprehension, I resigned from my CEO job at Lenox, and Reneé and I packed up our five kids and moved from the Philadelphia area to Seattle. I spent the next twenty years at World Vision traveling nearly three million miles and visiting some sixty countries, often with Reneé at my side. It turned out to be the great adventure of our lives.

Looking back on all these experiences, I can now see that God guided my life from the very start. As I fought to control my own destiny, even as a child, God was calling me to let go and trust him. As I reached for my dreams at Cornell and Wharton, God was preparing me to replace my dreams with his. And as I worked my way up the corporate ladder, God was teaching me to be faithful and to surrender to his purposes. Surrender is an unnatural act for most of us. We much prefer to be in control of our lives.

The apostle Paul observed that God's power is only made perfect through our weakness, which is a perplexing idea for a leader. It was at World Vision that I finally understood that concept: God's strength through our weakness. With a job description that involved confronting some of the oldest problems facing the

GOD'S POWER IS ONLY MADE PERFECT THROUGH OUR WEAKNESS, WHICH IS A PERPLEXING IDEA FOR A LEADER.

human race—poverty, famine, disease, conflict, ethnic hatred, human trafficking, and even genocide—my weaknesses and inadequacies were laid bare. I was in way over my head. That's when I finally and completely surrendered. And as a Christian leader surrender is the place where your leadership must begin.

SURRENDER

NOT MY WILL BUT THY WILL

SCRIPTURE ➤ "For whoever wants to save their life will lose it, but whoever loses their life for me will find it." (Matthew 16:25)

LEADERSHIP PRINCIPLE ➤ The starting point of Christian leadership is total surrender.

The greatest crisis we ever face is the surrender of our will.

OSWALD CHAMBERS

God takes that which is nothing and makes something out of it. When you become a Christian, you cannot patch your Christianity onto your old life. You are to start over. Accept God's call as a promotion. Burn the old bridges and fix it so you cannot go back; then serve God with all your heart.

A. W. TOZER

LEADERS NEVER SURRENDER. Leaders take control. Leaders are tough and demanding. Leaders never show weakness. These are the leadership truisms that I was taught in my years in corporate

33

▲

America, and they are still prevalent today. But these are not the ways of a follower of Jesus Christ. The Christian leader must march to a different drumbeat.

When you stop to think about it, so much of our Christian faith is paradoxical and even counterintuitive. Jesus had to die in order to bring us life. If we want to be great, we must first become servants. Out of our weakness God brings strength. And for the Christian leader, surrender is the prerequisite to any victory. In fact, the very act of becoming a Christian begins with total surrender. God wants us all in. He wants us to let go of everything we hold dear in our lives and lay those things at his feet and in his service. Only then are we truly useful to God. He doesn't accept a compartmentalized life in which our careers are held back and kept outside our total submission to his purposes.

But most of us don't want to cede control of our lives entirely. There are things we don't want to surrender and so we play games with God. "Lord, I will surrender most of my life, but I do have some conditions and exclusions." And we all have that list of things that we still want to control. It might be our work, money, time, lifestyle, family business, bad habit, or even the place we live. But God is not interested in negotiating our terms of surrender. He wants all of us. In the words of Oswald Chambers: "If you have only come as far as asking God for things, you have never come to the point of understanding the least bit of what surrender really means. You have become a Christian based on your own terms."

BENCHED BY GOD

I learned a lesson about the importance of surrender the hard way about ten years into my career. I had become so distracted by my professional ambitions that I had lost sight of my identity as an ambassador for Christ. Without fully realizing it, I had gradually compartmentalized my career and partitioned it off from the rest of my life. Becoming a CEO with all the trappings of money, status, recognition, and power was both intense and exhilarating. It became all-consuming in ways that forced other dimensions of my life to the margins. Apparently, to get my life back in balance, I needed to hit the reset button. So, God pulled me out of "the game" and sat me on the bench to spend a little time with the coach.

Two years after becoming CEO of Parker Brothers, I was unceremoniously fired. Because of steep earnings declines and general volatility in their toy businesses, General Mills, Parker Brothers' parent company, made the decision to spin off all its toy companies into a separate, publicly traded company. In doing so, they decided to replace most of the division presidents so they could present the new company to Wall Street with brand-new management teams. So, after my remarkably swift ascent, I experienced an even swifter fall. And it was incredibly painful.

Over the next two years I would find another job, move my family, get fired again, and spend a total of about fourteen months unemployed. I remember my wife saying to me, "Whatever lesson God is trying to teach you, please learn it soon so you can get back to work." God was indeed doing some business with me during that season. If I am brutally honest with myself, I had become somewhat enamored with the early success I had experienced. While my identity was that of a follower of Jesus Christ, my career was a part of my life that I tended to manage apart from God. Sure, I tried to be a good Christian in the workplace, but I hadn't fully connected the God I worshiped on Sunday to the work I did on Monday. And

Billy Gaston

Practical Atheist

I didn't truly understand how my responsibility to be an ambassador for Christ was supposed to take precedence in my life over all other priorities.

Being fired is humiliating. Most of us are deeply defined by the work that we do and the titles that we hold. So, when those things are taken away, we experience an identity crisis and a sense of grief and loss that shakes us to the core. But for me, being fired turned out to be the best way, maybe the only way, for God to get my attention. When you are "unwillingly unemployed," God has your complete, undivided attention. You feel helpless and powerless, which, as it turns out, is exactly the way God wants us to feel before him. Because when we feel powerful and in control of our lives, God has a hard time getting our attention.

During this painful season I had the longest and best devotional times of my life because I had absolutely no competing demands, and I was totally dependent on God because all of my support systems had been taken away. During those long months I did a lot of whining and crying out to God from my place of pain. "Why God—why did this happen? Help me, Lord, help me find another job. I have a family to support. Why me, Lord?" I didn't like the feeling of not being in control. Why was God sidelining me like this? It turns out that my painful identity crisis was exactly what God wanted me to experience.

The answer I had been looking for came to me one day during my prayer time in the form of a memory from my childhood. I had been raised Catholic, and I remembered having to study the catechism to prepare for my first Communion when I was about five or six years old. There were questions and answers we had to memorize, and the nuns would quiz us each week. One of those questions was simple and profound: "Why did God make you?" And thirty years after I had first memorized the answer, I still knew it. "God made me to know him, to love him, and to serve him in this life." It came back to me like a bolt of lightning. What had God called me to do at Parker Brothers? To know him, love him, and serve him in that place for as long as I was there. What was God calling me to do in my time of unemployment? To know him, love him, and serve him in that circumstance. And when I finally found another job, what would God be calling me to do there? You got it—to know him, love him, and serve him in that new place. Now this may sound ridiculously simplistic to you, but it is exactly what God expects of us. Once we are forgiven and transformed by the sacrifice of Christ, we become his possession; we are a new creation called to know, love, and serve him for the rest of our earthly lives. We are given a new identity, a new vocation. It was so simple. That was the lesson Reneé hoped I would learn from God. And it changed everything.

> **WE ARE A NEW CREATION CALLED TO KNOW, LOVE, AND SERVE CHRIST FOR THE REST OF OUR EARTHLY LIVES.**

A few months later—nine to be exact—I was hired by Lenox to run a small division. I was finally back to work. And I can still remember my prayer that first morning at my desk. "Lord, I am so grateful for this new work you have given me to do. Thank you! But, Lord, show me how I can know, love, and serve you here today in this place. I am not here to sell more china. I am not here to get raises and promotions. I am here for one purpose, to know,

1.) We have to understand our purpose.

SURRENDER TO CHRIST'S PURPOSES IS NOT JUST A ONE-TIME EVENT; IT'S A DAILY NECESSITY.

love, and serve you in the midst of the other people you have placed here with me." That was thirty-three years ago, and I have tried to live that prayer every day since. You see, if we want to truly devote our lives and our careers to Christ, surrender to his purposes is not just a one-time event; it's a daily necessity.

WE HAVE THIS ONE JOB

Have you ever visited a restaurant where the waiter seems to miss every single cue? You wait twenty minutes for him to come to your table, then another twenty before he takes your order. And the restaurant isn't even busy or understaffed. When the food finally comes you realize he got your orders all wrong and forgot your side of Brussels sprouts entirely. Filling your water glass—that's just a bridge too far. Then, to add insult to injury, he makes you wait twenty more minutes for the check, which includes a twenty percent service charge "for your convenience." Or maybe you've experienced that retail clerk who totally ignores you because she is on the phone with her girlfriend while you are waiting impatiently (in Christian love) to pay for your new Bible.

I know that more than once I have muttered under my breath the expression, "You had this one job—and you couldn't even do that?" It is usually something we say or think when someone who has a very clear job responsibility can't manage to do the one thing their job requires, usually because they either don't understand what their "one job" is or because they are so distracted with other things that they can't seem to do it.

Well, get ready for turnabout: I think that God may be muttering that same line under his breath when he looks at how we live out our faith. In a previous chapter I outlined in some detail the one job of every Christian to "join the revolution" that Jesus called the coming of the kingdom of God. The Great Commission, to make disciples of all nations, and the Great Commandment, to love our neighbors as ourselves, comprise the urgent assignment Jesus gave to his followers just before he left. They were commands, not suggestions—commands to join with him in reconciling the world to himself. God has begun the process of restoring his creation and setting the world right, and he has invited us to join him in this vocation as his ambassadors. This is, in fact, our one job, our holy calling, our new identity, and the single task he has given us to do. And yet, like the clueless waiter or distracted retail clerk, Christians often fail to take seriously that one job Christ has given them.

When we leave our churches on Sunday and enter our workplaces on Monday, there is an abrupt culture shock. The language is different, the values are different, and the content of our jobs often has nothing to do with our Christian faith. In fact, in secular workplaces there are often rules and policies forbidding religious dialogue in the office. It is easy to understand why we might leave Sunday behind and immerse ourselves in the very different demands and realities of our workplaces. And because we spend forty or more hours each week interacting at work, it is almost inevitable that our faith will become "walled off" and compartmentalized, unless we are intentional in avoiding that outcome. The result is that our very identity becomes fractured. We are followers of Jesus at home and at church, and something else altogether at work. We not only fail to perform our "one job," we even begin to lose our sense of identity as ambassadors of Christ.

WE ARE CALLED FOR A PURPOSE

We often get confused about how our careers, our vocations, intersect with our faith and our calling. But think of it this way. Your career is just the setting in which you live out your calling to serve as Christ's ambassador. You may be Christ's ambassador in a school, in a corporation, in a hospital, in government, or in your neighborhood. But the critical thing to keep straight is that your Christian calling to serve God in this life sits above your career or occupation. Like the hapless waiter in my earlier illustration, we have this one job. It has been given to us by God and it takes precedence over every other priority. In simple terms, that job is to know, love, and serve Christ by joining in his kingdom revolution to transform the world.

YOUR CAREER IS JUST THE SETTING IN WHICH YOU LIVE OUT YOUR CALLING TO SERVE AS CHRIST'S AMBASSADOR.

Are you familiar with the TV series *The Americans*—the one about a married couple living undercover in the United States in the 1980s as Soviet spies? They lived in suburbia, had two kids, and ran a travel agency. They seemed like a typical American family, but they weren't. The travel agency wasn't their real job. Their real job was to serve the Soviet Union and carry out its purposes, and they never allowed their "cover job" to distract them from their real job. They had surrendered their lives to a higher calling. Okay, the metaphor isn't perfect, but think of it this way: My real purpose at Lenox was to serve Jesus Christ by representing his interests there. I was "on assignment" there for Jesus, with the goal of furthering his kingdom and demonstrating his grace and love to the people I worked with. Making and selling fine china was just my cover.

THE SURRENDERED LEADER

But you may rightfully ask, What does this "surrender" stuff really have to do with leadership? How does it make a difference in my workplace? Here's my answer: A surrendered leader has nothing left to lose because they've already put everything in God's hands. There's nothing left to fear or protect. A surrendered leader can rise above the daily pressures and stresses of life and work. A surrendered leader is not bound by the same worries, concerns, and priorities that consume others. A surrendered leader is called to a higher purpose: to know, love, and serve God in this life. A surrendered leader looks and acts differently because it's no longer about them.

So, when coworkers look at a surrendered leader, they see something unusual, someone who marches to a different

A SURRENDERED LEADER HAS NOTHING LEFT TO LOSE BECAUSE THEY'VE ALREADY PUT EVERYTHING IN GOD'S HANDS.

drummer, someone whose life is about more than success, status, and money. They see a leader who tries to exemplify the qualities of Jesus: integrity, humility, encouragement, perseverance, courage, and forgiveness. This kind of leader values the well-being of the people in their care more than the urgent demands of the moment. This kind of leader provokes questions: Why do you seem different? Why do you care? What makes you tick? And the answers to those questions are found in the gospel, the good news that God loves them and that they too can embrace something bigger than themselves, something noble and pure and life-giving. This is how we bring Christ to the workplace and how people are drawn into the kingdom of God. This is how institutions and communities are shaped and made more pleasing to Christ. This is how the world changes. This is our one job. "For whoever wants to save their life will lose it, but whoever loses their life for me will find it" (Matthew 16:25).

SACRIFICE

CAREER SUICIDE

SCRIPTURE ➤ "As Jesus was walking beside the Sea of Galilee, he saw two brothers, Simon called Peter and his brother Andrew. They were casting a net into the lake, for they were fishermen. 'Come, follow me,' Jesus said, 'and I will send you out to fish for people.' At once they left their nets and followed him." (Matthew 4:18-20)

LEADERSHIP PRINCIPLE ➤ We must sacrifice our ambitions for Christ's ambitions for us.

> *He is no fool who gives what he cannot keep*
> *to gain that which he cannot lose.*
>
> **JIM ELLIOT**

> *If you yourself do not cut the lines that tie you to the dock,*
> *God will have to use a storm to sever them and to send you*
> *out to sea. Put everything in your life afloat upon God,*
> *going out to sea on the great swelling tide of his purpose.*
>
> **OSWALD CHAMBERS**

My wife advised me that starting a leadership book with chapters on surrender and sacrifice is not the most enticing way to motivate readers. I suspect that chapters on victory and reward would be much more appealing, but unfortunately those are benefits we are promised in the next life but not guaranteed in this one. Merriam-Webster offers these definitions for the word *sacrifice*: "an act of offering to a deity something precious; destruction or surrender of something for the sake of something else; something given up or lost."

These definitions really hit the mark. When we surrender our lives to God, it comes with a cost. There will be a real price to pay because we are replacing our ambitions, priorities, and dreams with his. God wants to repurpose us. And there will be moments when that sacrifice becomes very real and tangible. We need to remember Mother Teresa's profound observation that God has not called us to be successful but faithful—to put him first in our lives. And this applies to our careers as much as it does to the other dimensions of our lives.

LEAVING OUR NETS BEHIND

Consider the example of Peter and Andrew. They were brothers who were fishermen on the Sea of Galilee. They owned at least one boat and scratched out their living by catching fish and selling them in the marketplace. Jesus saw them at work and simply invited them: "Come, follow me." They were ordinary Jewish fishermen with little education and unlikely to be chosen to be disciples of any rabbi. But Jesus offered them the enigmatic promise that he would repurpose them and make them "fishers of men." Their response to his invitation is remarkable: "At once they left their nets and followed him" (Matthew 4:19-20). They dropped everything and immediately followed Jesus with no conditions and no questions asked. Earlier that day they had heard his teaching and had seen him perform a miracle on their own boat. And so, when Jesus invited them to join his inner circle, they embraced this higher calling without hesitation. They understood that following Jesus must take precedence over everything else in their lives.

We don't know the exact socioeconomic situation of Peter and Andrew, but we can assume they had families to support, and it is unlikely that they had a lot of money in the bank or 401(k)s set up for their retirement. But when Jesus called, they simply obeyed, trading their lives as fishermen for the uncertain promise of an itinerant preacher. "They pulled their boats up on shore, *left everything* and followed him" (Luke 5:11). They sacrificed everything to follow Jesus.

The immediate obedience of Peter and Andrew poses an uncomfortable question for us, doesn't it? Are we willing, without hesitation, to risk everything for our faith? That's the bar that Jesus sets for us. Jesus often spoke about the high cost of becoming his disciple. In the story of the rich young ruler, Jesus confronts another young man regarding his expectation of total commitment, but with a very different outcome.

As Jesus started on his way, a man ran up to him and fell on his knees before him. "Good teacher," he asked, "what must I do to inherit eternal life?"

"Why do you call me good?" Jesus answered. "No one is good—except God alone. You know the commandments: 'You shall not murder, you shall not commit adultery, you shall not steal, you shall not give false testimony, you shall not defraud, honor your father and mother.'"

"Teacher," he declared, "all these I have kept since I was a boy."

Jesus looked at him and loved him. "One thing you lack," he said. "Go, sell everything you have and give to the poor, and you will have treasure in heaven. Then come, follow me."

At this the man's face fell. He went away sad, because he had great wealth. (Mark 10:17-22)

Let's look at just a few elements of this powerful story. First, this young man was sincere in his faith. He wanted to do the right thing. He had kept the commandments and probably had tithed his income and faithfully practiced the weekly requirements of his synagogue. He was a good Jew. He was probably hoping for some affirmation and maybe even a high-five from this new rabbi he had traveled to see. But Jesus used the moment to show that he expects total surrender. Going through the motions of our faith is not the same thing as total commitment. God demands all of us. "One thing you lack,"

GOING THROUGH THE MOTIONS OF OUR FAITH IS NOT THE SAME THING AS TOTAL COMMITMENT.

he said. "Go, sell everything you have and give to the poor, and you will have treasure in heaven. Then come, follow me." You see, when we seek to follow Jesus, he wants much more than our church attendance, our 10 percent tithe, our Bible studies. He won't be compartmentalized—he wants everything we have. He wants us to die to our former self and to see that our sole purpose in life is to follow him. Jesus calls us to immediately leave our nets, holding nothing back. This is the kind of sacrifice he asks from us. Remember that definition? *Sacrifice: an act of offering to a deity something precious.*

"Everything" is a high price to pay, but Jesus is not a cruel master. He doesn't intend to strip us of all we have. He just wants us to acknowledge that everything we have and all we hope for are his to do with as he pleases. We are trusting him with those things by holding them loosely while letting him keep the deeds of ownership. There's nothing wrong with having career ambitions, wanting a comfortable home, and wanting to enjoy our lives with friends and family. He only asks that we always put him first, above our other priorities, and that we make all we have and all we are available to him.

This kind of commitment became real to me when I received the call from an executive recruiter asking whether I would be willing to leave my job at Lenox and come to World Vision. In the last chapter I told how I started my brand-new job at Lenox after months of unemployment. I was so grateful to God for bringing me through that wilderness period and into my "promised land." I had learned some valuable lessons about my walk with the Lord but now, at Lenox, I was "back in the game" and immediately immersed in my new role at a new company.

Fast-forwarding to ten years into my time at Lenox, I had prospered again, as I had at Parker Brothers, to become group president, then COO, and finally CEO of all of Lenox. God had shown me his blessings in that next season of my life, and I was riding high. Life was good, not just in my work life but in my family as well. Now with five children, Reneé and I had been blessed with a wonderful marriage and family. We had bought our dream house, an 1803 fieldstone farmhouse on five acres, and looked forward to raising our kids there.

So, when the phone rang one day and that executive recruiter presented me with the opportunity to quit my CEO job, take a huge pay cut, sell our home, and move my family across the country, I was less than enthusiastic. This certainly didn't fit into my plans. Had it been a call for almost any other job, I would have hung up. But this was no ordinary job and no ordinary recruiter. God was once again doing some business with me. He was asking whether I would literally be willing to sell everything I had, give it to the poor, and follow him.

I remember telling the recruiter emphatically that I was not qualified, not interested, and not available. World Vision was one of the largest Christian ministries in the world, helping more than one hundred million of the poorest people in the world every year with food, water, health, education, and economic opportunity. I knew absolutely nothing about global poverty. I had no nonprofit experience, no theological training, and no fundraising skills. Remember, my "expertise" had been in selling toys and games for children and expensive china for the wealthy—not exactly the perfect résumé to lead World Vision. Besides, I had a sizable mortgage to pay and five kids who needed orthodontics and a college education. I had worked hard for decades to get to the top of my profession, and quitting my job to go work for a ministry would effectively be career suicide.

I thought my arguments listing the reasons why World Vision wouldn't want me sounded pretty convincing. But midway through the call, that persistent recruiter changed tactics and asked me a bombshell of a question: "Rich, are you willing to be open to God's will for your life?" Okay, you really can't say no to that question, can you? But if you say yes, it takes you somewhere you don't want to go. You see, what he was really asking me was whether I had completely surrendered my life to Christ. Was I holding anything back? Was I ready to sacrifice—to leave my nets to follow him? Did I *really* understand the answer to that old catechism question, "Why did God make me?" I knew the correct response: to know him, to love him, and to serve him in this life. But was I ready and willing to do it? Wasn't I in the very same position as that rich young man who Jesus said lacked one thing?

That man's story ends with this devastating outcome: "At this the man's face fell. He went away sad, because he had great wealth." He couldn't do what Jesus asked and so he walked away in sadness, perhaps realizing that he did not have enough faith to literally surrender everything. I had the same visceral reaction that young man must have had. My face fell and I was very sad. Could I really walk away from everything I had worked for? Could I just abandon my career, leave my friends, sell my home, and move my family? Come on, Jesus, haven't I been a good Christian all these years? Do I really need to give you everything? "You lack one thing, Rich. Sell everything you have and give it to the poor. Then come, follow me." And like that rich young man, I nearly walked away, unwilling to give what Jesus was asking.

As I have written in a previous book, I did not accept the job with World Vision with great enthusiasm or with any sense of joy. Wracked with fear and uncertainty, I was no Christian superhero. It was the most difficult thing I had ever been asked to do. In the end, I did say yes, but mostly out of grudging obedience. That's why I admire so much the unflinching obedience of Peter and Andrew on that day when they immediately left their nets. They did not ask about salary and benefits. There was no hesitation over whether this would interrupt their fishing careers, interfere with their work-life balance, or require them to take too many risks. (They both later died as martyrs.) Instead, they saw the opportunity to serve God and align with his purposes in the world, and they were all in.

God will probably never ask you to literally sell everything you have and give it to the poor. But he does ask you to make that same kind of commitment to him even now. He wants you to take everything you have and all that you are and lay those things at his feet for him to do with them—and with you—as he chooses.

THE POTTER AND THE CLAY

In several places in the Bible God uses the metaphor of the potter and the clay. God is the potter, the one who is creating and shaping a vessel with his firm hands, and we are the clay.

> This is the word that came to Jeremiah from the LORD: "Go down to the potter's house, and there I will give you my message." So I went down to the potter's house, and I saw him working at the wheel. *But the pot he was shaping from the clay was marred in his hands; so, the potter formed it into another pot, shaping it as seemed best to him.*
>
> Then the word of the LORD came to me. He said, "Can I not do with you, Israel, as this potter does?" declares the LORD. "Like clay in the hand of the potter, so are you in my hand, Israel." (Jeremiah 18:1-6)

Now I happen to know a thing or two about pottery and clay because Lenox, the company I led for a decade, was America's premier "potter." Lenox manufactured several million pieces of beautiful pottery every year in three different factories and was honored to make the White House China used at formal state dinners since the days of Woodrow Wilson. At Lenox I learned how mere earth and clay are transformed into something both beautiful and useful.

The potter must first knead the clay under pressure into the exactly right consistency so that it can take and hold the desired shape. Then this raw, fragile, pressed clay must go into the furnace and be fired for many hours at temperatures above two thousand degrees to harden it and burn out any impurities. Those pieces that survive the ordeal without cracking are then carefully coated with a glaze of liquid glass and sent again into the brutal heat of the kiln for hours, emerging with the lovely gloss that characterizes the most beautiful china. But the process is still not complete. The potter must then bring the rather plain piece to life by painting it with vibrant colors and designs and then painstakingly embellishing it with brilliant twenty-four-karat gold. Then back it goes into the kiln again for yet more heat and more fire. Only then is the final work of art ready for service.

Pressure and heat. Pressure and heat. The potter's creation is subjected to pressure and heat again and again until its imperfections are burned out. Not all vessels will make the grade. The clay must surrender to the potter's touch. Clay that is too brittle—too unwilling to be shaped—or too pliable—too amorphous to hold a shape—will not survive the crucible.

Ordinary clay must be transformed to become the useful and pleasing vessel the potter intends. The clay must first die before a beautiful bowl or pitcher or vase can be born, just as we must die to self before we become useful and pleasing to Jesus. It requires us to sacrifice our ambitions in exchange for Christ's ambitions for us, trusting him as he shapes and works the clay of our lives toward his purposes. He wants to give us a new vocation, a new purpose as his ambassadors, sent out to demonstrate his love and his character to a watching world.

ORDINARY CLAY MUST BE TRANSFORMED TO BECOME THE USEFUL AND PLEASING VESSEL THE POTTER INTENDS.

TRUST

HE'S GOT THIS

SCRIPTURE ▷

"But blessed is the one who trusts in the LORD,
    whose confidence is in him.
They will be like a tree planted by the water
    that sends out its roots by the stream.
It does not fear when heat comes;
    its leaves are always green.
It has no worries in a year of drought
    and never fails to bear fruit." (Jeremiah 17:7-8)

[handwritten: InFAntcy to MAtority — trials]

LEADERSHIP PRINCIPLE ▷ Only by learning to trust God for their careers can leaders truly rise above the daily stresses and pressures of life and bear fruit for the Lord.

> *Trust is accepting what God sends into your life whether you understand it or not.*
>
> **TIM KELLER**

> *It is presumptuous in me to wish to choose my path, because I cannot tell which path is best for me. I must leave it to the Lord, who knows me, to lead me by the path which is best for me, so that in all things His will may be done.*
>
> **TERESA OF ÁVILA**

IT SHOULD FOLLOW LOGICALLY that once you have surrendered fully to God's will for your life and work that you can then trust God for the outcomes, right? He's got this. But life is hard. Work is hard. Office politics can be horrible; things aren't fair, layoffs happen, sometimes you have a terrible boss. And insecurity and worry can be the natural byproduct of all of this. Trusting God completely is one of the hardest things we are ever asked to do. But only by trusting God can you truly rise above the daily stresses and pressures of life and work. And it's when you manage to rise above these pressures that your coworkers see a different kind of leader, one who isn't rattled by the things that rattle everyone else. *Stonewall Jackson quote*

ONLY BY TRUSTING GOD CAN YOU TRULY RISE ABOVE THE DAILY STRESSES AND PRESSURES OF LIFE AND WORK.

A church of grace not Drama

Perhaps the best example of this mindset is Jesus himself. In the midst of the brutality of the Roman Empire, his rejection by the religious leaders of the day, the disbelief of his own disciples, and the real threat of physical violence against him, Jesus was calm, focused, and totally dependent on God his Father. And people followed him. He exuded a kind of peace and confidence that was as attractive as it was unusual. That's the way God wants us to live in relationship with him—as children trusting our Father.

I learned some vital lessons about trusting God early in my career. In my first job, I felt like my fledgling career was going nowhere. I had accepted a job right out of business school with Gillette. It was a job in sales administration that came with the promise that I could move into the marketing department (where I really wanted to be) after a year or two. But it turns out that promise was empty, and I was told after my first year that a transfer wouldn't be possible.

So, there I was, just twenty-five years old and my career dreams were already being derailed. I moped around for a few weeks and then finally updated my résumé. Reading the want ads one day in *Advertising Age*, I saw a one-inch-column ad from Parker Brothers Games for a marketing assistant position. Sweet, I thought, I could get into marketing and even get paid to play games. So I wrote a cover letter and sent off my first résumé. After a battery of interviews, I was offered the job! The next day I went into work and gave my two-week notice. What I didn't know was at that very moment, Gillette had been planning a major restructuring and layoff. And just a few days after giving my notice, I arrived at work to find panic and dread in the hallways. Two divisions were being merged, and everyone was told to sit at their desks and wait for a phone call. One by one, people were told whether they had been fired or retained. There was a bloodbath that day at Gillette, but I was immune. It reminded me of the story of Passover in Genesis, as the "angel of death" passed over my cubicle. I was protected because I had already resigned. I learned later that I would have been fired that day. I was the least senior person in my department and the one who would have been eliminated, but since I had just accepted the job at Parker Brothers, I was spared.

That night Reneé and I went to our couples' Bible study group, and I shared the dramatic events of the day. I shared that God had not only protected me from losing my job, but that he had given me an even better job—my dream job—at Parker Brothers. And then I said something to the group that turned out to be prophetic: "I learned something important in all of this," I said. "I really shouldn't worry about my career because God has my back. So, I can just relax and trust him with all that." And then I used some hyperbole as only a twenty-five-year-old can do: "If God wants me to someday become the president of Parker Brothers [a ridiculous notion at the time], then nothing on earth can stop him. And if he doesn't want me to become president of Parker Brothers, then there is nothing I can do to achieve it. So, my job is just to show up every day, do my best, and trust God for the outcome. I don't need to worry about this other stuff."

And that's what I did, truly believing that I could trust God for the outcome. It was an absolutely liberating feeling, to be freed from the inevitable anxieties of the workplace. Of course, being human, I did feel anxieties over the years ahead when things got tough, but that early experience of God's protection never left me. Over the next seven years at Parker Brothers, I was promoted on average once every nine months until I became president. It was almost as if God were saying to me: "Do you see what I can do, Rich, if you trust me?" And I would need that assurance over the years ahead as God would ask me to trust him again and again, even when trust was not easy.

As I have already shared, two years after becoming Parker Brothers' president, I was fired, found a new job, and was fired again. Trusting God in the good times was a lot easier than trusting him in the hard times. But I also learned that God was using those hard times to deepen my trust and reliance on him alone.

THE STRENGTH OF A TRUSTING LEADER

One thing people notice about a leader who trusts God is that they are able to remain calm in the face of adversity because they have a larger perspective on the daily turbulence of the workplace. I can remember many times in my career muttering the words, "This too shall pass." In the midst of some gut-wrenching upheavals at work, one of my coworkers and I would often look at each other and say, "In ten years when we look back, this crisis won't have mattered." And ten years later it hadn't. Our faith can and should provide us with a healthy perspective on the inevitable workplace crises.

During one particularly grim time at Lenox, when one of our divisions was going through an existential struggle that could easily have resulted in closing it down, I went to their offices for a financial review. I was the COO at the time and in a position of authority. I remember walking into the conference room where the division leadership was waiting for me and seeing the stricken look on their faces. They had been desperately working on plans to turn the division around and were very aware of the possibility that they might all lose their jobs. Their anxiety was almost palpable. And at that moment I just saw them as human beings, filled with fear and apprehension. I started by telling them to relax. We would have our business review in a few minutes, but first I wanted to just talk to them. I said something like this: "All of you are incredibly smart, talented, and hard-working leaders. I know you have done your best in the face of overwhelming odds. I don't know what decision will be made about whether your division will be closed or spared right now, but it's important to put all this in perspective. This is not the end of the world. We're selling porcelain figurines for heaven's sake. This is a time to hold on to the things that are much more important. You have families who love you. You have your health. You have talents that will make you desirable to any employer if things don't work out here, and no one can take those things away from you. We will all go through this together. And when you look back on this in ten years you will see this as just another bump in the road. So now let's jump into the business plan and see what we can do."

I just tried to say a few encouraging words. It didn't change the reality, but I could see the relief in their body language. I had helped them see past the trauma of the moment. As a Christian leader, I hadn't shared the gospel with them or done an altar call, but I had treated them as human beings precious to God and helped them through a tough time. I hopefully had made the workplace a little more pleasing to Christ as part of my "one job" to know, love, and serve God in this life.

ROOTED BY THE STREAM

Jeremiah compares the person who trusts their life to the Lord to "a tree planted by the water that sends out its roots by the stream."

> It does not fear when heat comes;
>> its leaves are always green.
> It has no worries in a year of drought
>> and never fails to bear fruit. (Jeremiah 17:7-8)

Notice that the tree is not spared the ravages of weather. Heat and drought come. The difference is how the tree, rooted by the water, is prepared for heat and drought. Its leaves stay green, and it still bears fruit.

But Jeremiah also speaks of those who fail to trust God:

> Cursed is the one who trusts in man,
>> who draws strength from mere flesh
>> and whose heart turns away from the LORD.
> That person will be like a bush in the wastelands;
>> they will not see prosperity when it comes.
> They will dwell in the parched places of the desert,
>> in a salt land where no one lives. (Jeremiah 17:5-6)

Pretty harsh. This person trusts in their own strength and abilities, which turns their heart away from the Lord. The result is compared to a bush in the wastelands—or, as Eugene Peterson renders this in *The Message*,

> He's like a tumbleweed on the prairie,
>> out of touch with the good earth.
> He lives rootless and aimless
>> in a land where nothing grows.

When Christians compartmentalize their faith from their work, they enter the workplace not as a tree with roots by the stream but like the tumbleweed, blown about by every crisis, out of touch with the life-giving God and unable to rise above worry to bear fruit where they are planted.

During that fiscal crisis at Lenox, I fought hard with my bosses to keep that struggling division open, and we found a way through the crisis. The division survived and ultimately returned to profitability. A few years later, when I left Lenox for World Vision, the same division president who looked so ashen that day was named the new CEO of Lenox. One of the vice presidents in the room that day was promoted to become the division's president. And I experienced yet another demonstration of the importance of trusting God in difficult times.

6

EXCELLENCE

IT'S HOW YOU PLAY THE GAME

SCRIPTURE ➤ "Whatever you do, work at it with all your heart, as working for the Lord, not for human masters, since you know that you will receive an inheritance from the Lord as a reward. It is the Lord Christ you are serving." (Colossians 3:23-24)

LEADERSHIP PRINCIPLE ➤ Excellence is not about winning; it's about producing the best result we are capable of achieving.

Doing our Best because our best is worth Doing.

> For when the One Great Scorer comes
> To mark against your name,
> He writes—not that you won or lost—
> But how you played the Game.

GRANTLAND RICE

THE PREMISE OF THIS BOOK is that the values leaders embrace are more important than the success they achieve. And yes, I understand that this statement flies in the face of virtually all the conventional wisdom permeating our success-driven culture. I am sure that for many of my readers, this point of view may come across as both naive and out of touch because your experience in the real world is that successful outcomes matter a great deal. So, I want to be clear in stating that *outcomes do matter*. But it is how those results are best achieved that matters more in the long run. Let me explain.

When the sole focus of an organization is placed on delivering outcomes, it can create an unhealthy culture in which the ends often justify the means. The bottom line starts to matter more than the people or the process working to deliver it. Bad behavior might get rewarded if the results of that behavior are positive. And this can create its own set of problems.

One extreme example of this is the Wells Fargo phony account scandal. Starting in 2011, aggressive goals were set by Wells Fargo senior management for their sales agents to increase the number of banking products and accounts their customers were enrolled in. Heavy pressure was applied to these agents to deliver, and punitive actions were taken if they didn't. As a result of this pressure, agents began to create phony accounts for their customers in order to meet their aggressive quotas. As many as two million such accounts were created, and many of their unwitting customers were charged millions of dollars in fees and experienced devastating hits to their credit ratings for accounts they didn't even know they had. When the scam was exposed, Wells Fargo was found guilty of fraud by regulators and required to pay millions of dollars in fines. Ultimately their CEO was forced to step down. This is an extreme example of what can happen when leaders take a "perform or perish" approach to delivering bottom-line outcomes, focusing strictly on the ends with little regard for the means.

But there are other problems with an unhealthy focus on outcomes. Sometimes that approach rewards mediocrity while punishing excellence. For example, consider two different teams in an organization. One team (with some luck and favorable circumstances) might deliver successful results despite making only mediocre efforts, while the other team (due to circumstances beyond their control) makes an outstanding effort that fails to deliver the desired results. In an outcome-focused culture we will reward the team that put forth the mediocre effort while punishing the team that worked with excellence. Here's what we miss: *good outcomes do not lead to excellence; excellence leads to good outcomes.* We need to reward excellence. We can't always control the outcomes of our work, but we can control the effort we put forth and celebrate those who work with diligence.

EXCELLENCE IS NOT ABOUT WINNING; IT'S ABOUT PRODUCING THE BEST RESULT WE ARE CAPABLE OF ACHIEVING.

Excellence is not about winning; it's about producing the best result we are capable of achieving. A commitment to excellence simply means that we will strive to do our very best and expect the same of others. This leads to a culture that rewards effort rather than outcome. In Christian terms, excellence means that we will always strive to use the gifts and abilities that God has given us to the fullest extent possible.

A PARABLE ABOUT EFFORT

In Matthew 25 we read the parable of the talents, in which the master gives a different amount of money to each of his three servants to manage before he leaves on a journey. One servant receives five talents, the second two talents, and the third one talent—"each according to his ability." When the master returns, he asks each servant what he has done with the money he was entrusted with. The one with five talents had produced five more, and the one with two talents produced two more, but the servant with one talent simply hid the money and did nothing to multiply it. The master rewards the first two servants with the words, "Well done, good and faithful servant! You have been faithful over a few things; I will put you in charge of many things. Come and share your master's happiness!" (Matthew 25:21, 23). But he is angry with the third servant, who did not produce more: "You wicked, lazy servant! So you knew that I harvest where I have not sown and gather where I have not scattered seed? Well then, you should have put my money on deposit with the bankers, so that when I returned I would have received it back with interest. So take the bag of gold from him and give it to the one who has ten bags" (Matthew 25:26-28).

It's common to see this as a "performance" parable where what mattered most were the outcomes. But it is actually a parable about effort. The master realized that the servants did not have equal abilities, and he gave them the different amounts based on their relative capabilities. What pleased the master about the first two servants was their effort and their diligence. They had both done their best, and they both received the same reward even though one had greater abilities and had managed a larger sum. The third servant was chastised because he made no effort at all. He hadn't even made the minimal effort of depositing the money in the bank to earn interest. The master was not rewarding the outcomes; he was rewarding the diligence and effort of the first two servants. Of course, this parable is not about money at all—it's about God's expectation that we will do our best to faithfully use the gifts we have been entrusted with on our Master's behalf.

When my kids were in high school, we had predictable clashes over their study habits and their grades. If there was a chemistry test in the morning, Mom and Dad didn't think that playing video games or watching TV the night before was the wisest choice—even if you thought chemistry was "stupid," as most of my kids did. I always told them that I didn't care what grade they got on the test but only that they did their very best. "All you can do is the best you can do," was my slogan. If you have done your best, I really can't ask any more of you. But watching TV the night before the test didn't cut it as doing their best.

When you think about it, the understanding that "all we can do is the best we can do" is incredibly liberating. If our best efforts fail, then they fail—no regrets. Once we have done our best, once we have "left it all on the field," we can have a clear conscience and accept the outcome.

A CELEBRATION CULTURE

There is some interesting psychology here. When the focus of a leader is only on the result, failure to achieve that result becomes an indictment of the team or the individual. It leads to shame and discouragement. But when the emphasis is on making our best effort, we can still celebrate the efforts of the individual or the team even in the midst of a failure. However, if I have given my best effort and I am punished because it did not deliver the desired outcome, I am in effect being punished for giving my best effort. The result is discouragement and shame, which will probably hurt my future performance. Conversely, if my best efforts are praised, even though I didn't achieve a successful outcome, I am motivated to continue to offer my best efforts in the future.

A focus solely on outcomes can lead to a shame culture, while a focus on best efforts creates a celebration culture. In a shame culture, people are blamed for poor outcomes even when they have worked tirelessly and done their best. When leaders create a celebration culture, they are using positive motivation by rewarding the right behaviors. Brené Brown in her bestselling book *Daring Greatly* speaks to the ways shame can smother a workplace: "If we want to reignite innovation and passion, we have to rehumanize work. When shame becomes a management style, engagement dies. When failure is not an option, we can forget about learning, creativity and innovation."

Pete Carroll, the winning coach of the Seattle Seahawks, has become known for his philosophy of coaching. Unlike many of the stern, authoritarian coaches we see stalking the sidelines every Sunday, Carroll is an exuberant cheerleader for his team. When asked about the importance of winning, Carroll said this: "Of course we want to win every game but *winning forever* is more about realizing your potential and *making yourself as good as you can be*. Realizing that is a tremendous accomplishment, whether it's in football or in life." Coach Carroll is saying that it's about each of his players doing their best—becoming the best they can be. Yes, the outcome is important, but the outcome starts with excellence—"making yourself as good as you can be." Pete Carroll has created a celebration culture within his team, not a shame culture, and it has helped them amass a ten-year record of one hundred wins versus fifty-seven losses and two trips to the Super Bowl, winning one of them.

Contrast this positive culture with the Houston Astros baseball cheating scandal, where the coaches and the players conspired to illegally "steal" pitching signals from the opposing catcher using video cameras so that their batters would know what pitch was coming next. This unfair advantage helped them win the 2017 World

Series. When the culture tells you that winning is everything, it can motivate some very destructive behaviors.

The famous quote by sportswriter Grantland Rice captures the essence of this principle: "It's not whether you win or lose, it's how you play the game." If we play hard, fair, and with passion and commitment, that's ultimately what matters more than winning. And teams that play that way every day will consistently win more games in the long run. The best leaders create a culture of excellence and set a high bar for achievement based not exclusively on outcomes but on fairness, commitment, and effort.

FORTY THOUSAND WINNERS

More than forty thousand people run in the Chicago Marathon each year, but there is only one male and one female winner. Does that mean that there are more than forty thousand losers? It does if winning is the only goal. In reality very few runners actually expect to win the marathon, but every runner is trying to achieve a personal best. It's all about their effort. For some, doing their best just means finishing. Others are thrilled with a five- or six-hour time even though the winner will run the race in just over two hours.

While I have never run in the Chicago Marathon, my son Andy ran it three times, and my son Pete ran once supporting World Vision's running ministry, Team World Vision. One year, Reneé and I went to cheer them on and watched as thousands of exhausted runners joyfully crossed the finish line. And what we saw was celebration. Thousands of people, each with their own unique story, were celebrating their achievement. They had run with perseverance and heart. They had made their best effort and they were exuberant. If winning had been the only acceptable outcome, more than forty thousand people would have gone home discouraged and defeated. But instead, they went home as winners because they had run hard and done their very best. Excellence is not about winning; it's about producing the best result we are capable of achieving.

GOOD ENOUGH IS NOT GOOD ENOUGH

When I left the corporate world to join World Vision, I went from a for-profit secular organization to a not-for-profit Christian ministry. The cultures were completely different. In my corporate jobs, outcomes were everything. They were typical "perform or perish" cultures where profit, or shareholder value, was king. Everyone had scorecards and deliverables, and everyone's bonus was based on achieving those results. Failure had consequences, from loss of compensation up to and including termination. It could be brutal at times.

But at World Vision I found a different ethic. There the culture was shaped around embracing the inspirational cause of helping the poor and World Vision's unique approaches to accomplishing it. Relationships were important in the culture, and people took great pride in identifying with the organizational mission, vision, and values. But in this Christian nonprofit organization, I found that money, or revenue, was seen more as the means to the end rather than the end in itself. That subtle difference led to less attention on some of the financial goals of the organization.

While World Vision US was right in not placing the total emphasis on financial outcomes, it had also not placed a strong enough emphasis on accountability and excellence in their fundraising. There weren't clear goals, scorecards, or metrics in place that were visible to the entire organization. I dubbed this the "we're good people doing good things and that's good enough" culture. Don't get me wrong, World Vision was doing some amazing work all around the world and helping millions of people. But I felt they had not created a culture of excellence around their fundraising and financial goals.

For those of you reading this who may be working in a Christian ministry context, this may sound familiar. Sometimes striving for excellence is seen as a "worldly" aspiration that feels inconsistent with Christian values such as kindness, forgiveness, and unity. When you're praying with someone in the morning, it's hard to give them a difficult performance review in the afternoon, even if they're failing at their job. But, when real performance issues aren't being addressed, it can result in dysfunction in the organization. A culture of excellence is not contrary to Christian values; it is actually central. If we are Christ's ambassadors in our workplaces and communities, the stakes are high. We are called to do our best because we carry with us the reputation of Christ: "Whatever you do, work at it with all your heart, as working for the Lord, not for human masters, since you know that you will receive an inheritance from the Lord as a reward. It is the Lord Christ you are serving" (Colossians 3:23-24).

During my first weeks at World Vision I began to address the issues of accountability and excellence. We did a deep dive on clarifying the mission, vision, and values of our fundraising organization. Then we established financial goals and metrics captured in both an organizational scorecard as well as individual scorecards. All these new initiatives understandably sent some shockwaves through the culture, and I started to hear some rumblings. My human resources VP shared with me that people were saying things like: "We're now being run like a Fortune 500 corporation—I thought we were a ministry." I felt I needed to address these issues at an all-staff meeting. I spoke to our staff saying that yes, if excellence and accountability are hallmarks of a Fortune 500 corporation, then I am guilty as charged. If excellence is expected of us when we work in a for-profit business, like Microsoft or Procter & Gamble, then how much more should we strive for excellence when we are serving God? I said that I wanted World Vision to be a model for excellence that even the Fortune 500 would admire. Most people enthusiastically embraced the new mentality because they wanted to do more and do better for the people we served. But a few chose to leave rather than adapt.

Over the next ten years World Vision's revenue tripled, and efficiency improved as overheads were reduced by a third. This wasn't because of any brilliance on my part. It happened because we released the pent-up potential in our people by creating a culture that celebrated excellence and embraced accountability to be the best we could be. This resulted in a massive amount of money being released into our ministry with the poor. Millions more people received improved nutrition, better health, clean water, education, and microloans to start their own businesses. This was not because we focused like a laser on outcomes but because we focused on excellence, the best results our people were capable of achieving. Good outcomes do not lead to excellence; excellence leads to good outcomes.

GOOD OUTCOMES DO NOT LEAD TO EXCELLENCE; EXCELLENCE LEADS TO GOOD OUTCOMES.

LOVE

WHAT'S LOVE GOT TO DO WITH IT?

SCRIPTURE ➤ "Love is patient, love is kind. It does not envy, it does not boast, it is not proud. It does not dishonor others, it is not self-seeking, it is not easily angered, it keeps no record of wrongs. Love does not delight in evil but rejoices with the truth. It always protects, always trusts, always hopes, always perseveres." (1 Corinthians 13:4-7)

LEADERSHIP PRINCIPLE ➤ Jesus calls us to love our neighbors as ourselves, and that includes our coworkers. When people see that their leader truly cares about them, it creates a relationship of trust, fosters a positive culture, and amplifies that leader's witness for Christ.

Nobody cares how much you know until they know how much you care.

TEDDY ROOSEVELT

I AM GUESSING THAT FOR MANY OF YOU reading this chapter right now, *love* is not the leadership quality that first comes to mind when you think of the attributes of a great leader. Courage, yes; excellence, yes; vision, yes; integrity, yes; perseverance, yes—but love? Really? At the office? What's love got to do with it? Everything.

Laws to Judgement And Hate

Legalism

Stephanie

What I want you to take away from this chapter is that in order to be an effective ambassador for Christ in your workplace, you need to see the people you work with from God's perspective—as people whom he loves, people for whom Jesus gave his life. Moreover, when those people look at you, they need to see a person who truly cares about them. Why? Because there is no more powerful witness to the truth of the gospel than Christ's love shining through us. As Christ's ambassadors we are called to embody the values and character of the one who sent us. We are to be the tangible demonstration of the love of Christ, the character of Christ, and the truth of Christ as we live out our faith publicly in full view of others.

The entire Bible is essentially a love story. It's the story of a loving God who pursued us so passionately that he was willing to send his Son to die for us that we might finally be reconciled to our Father in heaven. Perhaps the boldest and simplest statement about the centrality of love to our Christian faith comes in Matthew 22:35-40, when Jesus is asked by an expert in the Jewish law a provocative and clarifying question: "What is the greatest commandment in the Law?" Jesus answered: "'Love the Lord your God with all your heart and with all your soul and with all your mind.' This is the first and greatest commandment. And the second is like it: 'Love your neighbor as yourself.' All the Law and the Prophets hang on these two commandments."

This is a breathtaking statement. In a world where missional clarity is thought to be critical for every organization, Jesus is providing it here. He is essentially saying that if you take the entirety of the Old Testament law, if you summarize God's hope for the human race and distill that down to its core, it comes down to this: *love God and love other people—always.* If you need clarity about the essence of your Christian faith and what being a follower of Jesus entails, this is it, and it doesn't require a seminary degree. A Christian is called to love God and love other people always. That's what love has to do with it.

And did you notice the connecting phrase between these two commands, "the second is *like* it"? In other words, loving our neighbor as ourselves is *like*—the same as, a corollary to, inseparable from—loving God with all our heart, soul, and mind. This command, to love our neighbors as ourselves, known as the Great Commandment, envisions that we as Jesus' followers will actually demonstrate God's infinite love for people in tangible ways, not just with words and platitudes. We will make love part of our "operating system," both in life and in our leadership roles.

As a Christian leader, your coworkers should be among the main objects of your love of neighbor. While loving our coworkers is not always an easy thing to do, it's a very easy thing to understand. When you love someone as you love yourself, you look out for them, treat them with care, want the best for them, and are even willing to put their interests ahead of your own. It's about showing people that you value them, respect them, and care about their lives and careers. Paul describes this kind of love in 1 Corinthians: "Love is patient, love is kind. It does not envy, it does not boast, it is not proud. It does not dishonor others, it is not self-seeking, it is not easily angered, it keeps no record of wrongs. Love does not delight in evil but rejoices with the truth. It always protects, always trusts, always hopes, always perseveres" (1 Corinthians 13:4-7).

> AS A CHRISTIAN LEADER, YOUR COWORKERS SHOULD BE AMONG THE MAIN OBJECTS OF YOUR LOVE OF NEIGHBOR.

Even though this is a passage frequently read at weddings, it is also a startling description of what love ought to look like in a leader. Let me take some liberty here by substituting "I" for the word *love* to make this into a code of conduct for leaders. It doesn't change the meaning, but it makes it more personal: "As a leader: I am patient, I am kind. I do not envy, I do not boast, I am not proud. I do not dishonor others, I am not self-seeking, I am not easily angered, I keep no record of wrongs. I do not delight in evil but rejoice with the truth. I always protect, always trust, always hope, always persevere."

How's that for a leadership mantra? If you recited that in the mirror each morning before work, it might positively impact every encounter you have for the rest of the day. If you've ever served under a leader who acts like this, even a little bit, you are a fortunate person.

SHOW THEM YOU CARE

Loving our coworkers as ourselves needs to start with a paradigm shift in our perspective toward them. After about ten years of helping the world's poorest people as the leader of World Vision, I received a "lightning bolt" of spiritual insight about how God wanted me to see the poor. For years I operated under the assumption that God wanted me to help the poor because *he* loved the poor so much. So, helping the poor was my duty as a Christian. But I actually had it backward. God wanted me first to *love* the poor as he did because he knew that if I loved them, then I would do everything in my power to help them. The love had to come first. That's why we are all more passionate about seeing our own child succeeding in school or sports than someone else's child. We start with the foundation that we love our children. Once you love someone, everything else flows from that.

Most leaders at least give lip service to wanting to help their co-workers develop their skills, grow their capabilities, and achieve greater success. But what if you as a leader first loved them and saw them as people made in the image of God as Christ calls you to do? Then your advocacy on their behalf would be so much more genuine and passionate. The people you work with aren't your children, but they are God's children and are therefore worthy of your love.

Teddy Roosevelt's statement, "Nobody cares how much you know until they know how much you care," is quite accurate. I often say that no leader can really command respect because true respect must be earned. You can command obedience but not respect. When you show the people around you that you care, you earn the right to be their leader. People begin to respect you and trust you when they see that you care about them, their ideas, their opinions, their aspirations, and their lives outside the workplace. When you truly care about the people around you, and show your care in tangible ways, you will be amazed at how willingly they respond to your leadership.

> **WHEN YOU SHOW THE PEOPLE AROUND YOU THAT YOU CARE, YOU EARN THE RIGHT TO BE THEIR LEADER.**

HOW ABOUT THE UNLOVABLE?

But what about that awful person at work who is particularly heinous and unlovable—maybe even kind of despicable? This might be a person who has done hurtful things to you or others—a disruptive and selfish person who is just out for themselves. They may be the antithesis of the kind of love we just read about in 1 Corinthians. Isn't it a bit much to believe that (a) you could actually love someone like this and (b) it would make any difference? Well, Jesus did tell us to love our enemies: "You have heard that it was said, 'Love your neighbor and hate your enemy.' But I tell you, love your enemies and pray for those who persecute you" (Matthew 5:43-44).

I have a story to tell that is far removed from a workplace context or even an American context. But it illustrates the power unleashed when we love the unlovable and forgive the unforgivable. The story takes place in Lebanon in the midst of the Syrian refugee crisis, which drove hundreds of thousands of desperate Syrians across the Lebanese border to seek asylum. To appreciate what happened there, you first have to understand the context.

In 1976, during the Lebanese civil war, the Syrian army invaded Lebanon and occupied the country on and off for thirty years. They exerted total military control over the Lebanese people. They assassinated their prime minister. They raped their women and plundered their homes. Just imagine living for thirty years under the thumb of such a brutal regime. The Lebanese people hated their Syrian oppressors. And Syria did not withdraw from Lebanon until 2005.

Then, just six years later, the Syrian civil war broke out with violence. Now, hundreds of thousands of Syrians, mostly Muslim, fled toward the Lebanese border seeking refuge from the violence and persecution in their own country, desperately begging the Lebanese people for help. Now the tables had turned. It was payback time. "Love our enemies? I don't think so." Isn't that how we might have felt in the same situation?

On each of my trips to Lebanon I met with some Lebanese church pastors because I wanted to understand whether and how their churches were responding to the influx of Syrian refugees. One of them explained it this way: "Syria is our enemy. My father died in the war, our house was hit by bombs. Women were raped. *These are our enemies, not just people we don't like.*"

Put yourself in his position. Not only are these the same people who had persecuted you for thirty years, they are also Muslim, not even of the same faith. So, let me ask you, in these same circumstances, what do you think your church would do?

What many of the Lebanese churches did was both shocking and unexpected. They welcomed their former adversaries. Listen to what one of these pastors said to me: "When our church started assisting refugees, even the Syrians were surprised. 'Why are you helping them?' people asked. Our response is this: Because of the love of Christ we carry in our hearts, we assist them. We don't care what happened in the past, we tell the refugees. 'We care about the well-being of you and your children.' These are humans like we are. *We must surround them with the love of Christ.* You can't blame people for escaping bombings or wanting a better life. If you reach out to refugees, you turn them into good citizens. *Love never fails you. If you love honestly, an enemy will turn into a friend.*"

A few days later I attended the Sunday service at one of these remarkable churches. I stood there with tears in my eyes as I witnessed hundreds of Muslim refugees streaming into the church service— men, women, and children, young and old—responding to the love they had been shown, hungry to feel God's love for them, and hungry to learn about a Savior who loved them so much that he died for them. The love they felt was most powerful because it was unearned and unconditional.

That nasty coworker in the next cubicle from you may not deserve to be loved. He may have said some terrible things to you and about you. But his behavior probably doesn't rise to the level of Syrian oppressor. Instead of paying back insult for insult and offense with offense, try interacting with him in a positive and caring way—the same way you might treat someone who is kind and affirming toward you. It will get his attention, and in some cases it will even begin to change his behavior toward you. "But to you who are listening I say: Love your enemies, do good to those who hate you, bless those who curse you, pray for those who mistreat you. . . . Do to others as you would have them do to you. If you love those who love you, what credit is that to you? Even sinners love those who love them. And if you do good to those who are good to you, what credit is that to you? Even sinners do that" (Luke 6:27-28, 31-33).

WHAT WOULD LOVE DO?

I realize that all this talk about love can seem very abstract. So, what might it look like in practice where you work? Here are a few tips for putting the abstract into practice.

I think it starts when you embrace the proposition that God really does want you to demonstrate his love to the people you interact with every day. And it helps if you begin regularly praying for them during your prayer time. Try to approach people at work with a loving spirit. When you look at someone, do you have a glass-half-empty or a glass-half-full attitude toward them? Do you tend to see a person's flaws and shortcomings first, or their better attributes? If you can make it a practice to see the best in people rather than their shortcomings, they will feel more valued and respected. We all have shortcomings, but no one wants to be defined by those things. If you always see someone as deficient, they will begin to see themselves as deficient, and it may become self-fulfilling. But if you affirm someone's better qualities, they may rise to meet those higher expectations.

IF YOU AFFIRM SOMEONE'S BETTER QUALITIES, THEY MAY RISE TO MEET THOSE HIGHER EXPECTATIONS.

Don't put value labels on people. It helped me to always try to see people without their title or rank. The janitor was as worthy of care and respect as the CEO. And the CEO was just another human being who needed God's love as much as anyone else. Rank and title should not determine how you treat people in the workplace—or anywhere else. An attitude of superiority toward others will kill your witness for Christ at work.

Perhaps the most striking thing about Jesus' interaction with people is the way he treated those on the lowest rungs of the social ladder: the poor, the sick, prostitutes, lepers, tax collectors, women, and children. He showed them love and acceptance instead of disdain and rejection. In fact, he got in trouble

TAKE TIME TO SHOW THAT YOU VALUE THOSE WHO MIGHT FEEL DEVALUED.

with the Jewish elite for being so kind to the down-and-outs. In your workplace, take time to show that you value those who might feel devalued.

Get to know people. How much do you really know about the people on your team? Do you know the names of their kids? Do you know what's going on in their lives outside work, what their passions are? Are they caring for an aging parent or raising a child with special needs? People's lives are not one-dimensional. They are so much more than just a box on an organizational chart. When you, as a leader, make the effort to get to know the people around you at a deeper level, they feel valued and affirmed, and you gain a new appreciation for their unique gifts and abilities. this helps with ELOGG AND STAFF connections

Last, one of your key responsibilities as a leader is to help the people under your care realize their God-given potential. Take time to understand their hopes and aspirations and then work to help them achieve them. The best leaders help people achieve the things that are important to them through coaching, encouragement, and practical direction. I feel great satisfaction that more than a dozen of the people who worked for me at World Vision have gone on to become CEOs of other ministries and organizations. And many others have assumed larger responsibilities within World Vision. Going back to the orchestra-conductor metaphor: work to bring the music out of the people in your care.

Jesus' command to love our neighbors as ourselves is one of the hardest things to consistently obey—especially where we work. Every place I have ever worked was stressful. Work required people to perform under pressure, achieve tangible goals, navigate the constant friction of daily human interactions, and do so in an environment rife with workplace politics. The phrase "it's a jungle out there" is often an apt descriptor. Nevertheless, we are commanded by Jesus to love our coworkers—something not easy to do consistently.

Maybe this final thought will help you. Years ago, a lot of kids were wearing WWJD ("What would Jesus do?") bracelets. They served as a reminder to be more like Jesus by asking that simple question in every situation. But trying to set the standard of doing what God himself would do was an awfully high bar. In 1 John 4:8 we are given the shortest definition of God in the Bible: "God is love." If this is true, we can ask ourselves the more tangible question, "What would *love* do?" When you are about to give someone a difficult performance review, ask what *love* would say. When someone makes a mistake in their work, how would *love* react? When revenues are declining, profits are down, and staff are anxious, how would *love* behave? When one of your employees discovers they have cancer, what would *love* require? Try to keep that question on your lips in every encounter.

And before you show up at work tomorrow, try reciting these words: "As a leader: I am patient, I am kind. I do not envy, I do not boast, I am not proud. I do not dishonor others, I am not self-seeking, I am not easily angered, I keep no record of wrongs. I do not delight in evil but rejoice with the truth. I always protect, always trust, always hope, always persevere."

Because that's what love would do.

HUMILITY

THE EXECUTIVE TOILET

SCRIPTURE ➤ "Do nothing out of selfish ambition or vain conceit. Rather, in humility value others above yourselves, not looking to your own interests but each of you to the interests of the others." (Philippians 2:3-4)

LEADERSHIP PRINCIPLE ➤ A leader with humility understands that it's not about them. The humble leader listens to the input of others, encourages competing points of view, values all members of their team, and seeks the welfare of others over self.

True humility is not thinking less of yourself; it is thinking of yourself less.

RICK WARREN

GOD TAUGHT ME A RATHER HUMOROUS LESSON about humility on my first day as CEO of Lenox. After eight years of hard work, I had finally been promoted to the top job, and this was the day I would occupy the luxurious corner office for the very first time. It had a desk as big as a battleship, original paintings on the wall, and—wait for it—its own private executive bathroom. I remember getting up early that first day because I couldn't wait to get to work. And so, I arrived around seven, before anyone else on my wing was there. I sat at that imposing desk for the first time and opened my Bible for a quiet time with the Lord, praying that he would guide me and support me in my new responsibilities. I was feeling quite pleased about my new status.

But after my first cup of coffee, nature called, so I walked proudly into my gleaming new executive bathroom, yet another symbol that I had finally "arrived." And that's when it happened. When I flushed, I saw with dread in my heart that the water was not going down, it was rising. I had plugged the toilet. My next anxious flush (a rookie mistake) made it even worse, as the water started to crest toward the rim. That's when panic set in. How mortifying to have to tell my administrative assistant to call the maintenance department because the brand-new CEO had plugged his toilet. That story would spread around the building like wildfire.

But wait, I wasn't sunk yet; my racing mind had an idea. I dashed to my door and looked both ways to see if anyone had arrived. Not yet—whew! I ran down the hallway opening every closet door I could find, looking for the one object that might rescue me from humiliation—a plunger. Nothing in the first closet, so I ran to the second. Nothing in the second closet either. Panic! But in the third closet, I struck pay dirt: sitting in the far corner was a glorious plunger! Hallelujah! I grabbed it, peeked surreptitiously out the door, looked both ways again, and ran back to my office, safely closing the door behind me. I was almost home. After a few tries, the plunger worked its magic, and the toilet flushed. Relief washed over me. . . . that is until I realized that I was still holding the plunger in my hand. Now I had to get rid of the "murder weapon." And so, I repeated my frantic routine of spying out the hallway and then rushing down the corridor to the closet to redeposit the incriminating plunger.

When I finally got safely back to my desk I collapsed into my chair, sweating profusely but relieved. And then I literally laughed out loud. I don't know if God plays practical jokes on us, but I'm pretty sure he was behind this one. "Lord, apparently on my big day, you felt that I needed a little bit of humbling." I felt like God was saying to me, "Okay, Mr. Bigshot, yes, you're the CEO now, but just remember that you are no different and no more special than anyone else who works at Lenox. I am the one who placed you there, and if you become too full of yourself, I can also take you out."

This silly little episode served as a vivid reminder to me of the sin of pride, which can so easily rear its ugly head as we experience success. This is why humility in a leader is an all-too-rare quality. Rick Warren, in *The Purpose Driven Life*, said this of humility: "True humility is not thinking less of yourself; it is thinking of yourself less." I resonate with the truth of this statement because it suggests that humility does not require us to deny the positive gifts and talents we possess but rather to recognize that those gifts and talents are given to us by God for a purpose. Are you creative, charismatic, eloquent, intuitive, intelligent, politically astute? If you are any of those things it is because God has bestowed those gifts on you. And they have been entrusted to you to steward in ways that bring glory to God and further his purposes, not to use for your own glory and self-aggrandizement.

A leader's first responsibility is the well-being of the people he or she is entrusted to lead. Think again of a coach or a symphony conductor. Their job is to bring the best out of the players or musicians in their care. The second greatest commandment, to love our neighbors as ourselves, suggests that we as leaders must care as much about the welfare of those we lead as we do our own.

There is a passage in Deuteronomy that addresses this very real tendency toward pride as we experience success and prosperity. God, through Moses, gave a strong admonition to the Israelites just before they entered the Promised Land, reminding them of their total dependence on God. Remember, they had just spent forty years wandering in the wilderness with God sustaining them by miraculously providing them with manna every single day—for more than fourteen thousand days! One would think that the message of dependence on God would have sunk in by then. But Moses wanted to make sure they had learned the lesson. Moses warns them not to become arrogant as they transition from the ordeal of the wilderness to the prosperity of the Promised Land and to remember the one who led them there.

> When you have eaten and are satisfied, praise the LORD your God for the good land he has given you. Be careful that you do not forget the LORD your God, failing to observe his commands, his laws and his decrees that I am giving you this day. Otherwise, when you eat and are satisfied, when you build fine houses and settle down, and when your herds and flocks grow large and your silver and gold increase and all you have is multiplied, then *your heart will become proud and you will forget the LORD your God*, who brought you out of Egypt, out of the land of slavery. He led you through the vast and dreadful wilderness, that thirsty and waterless land, with its venomous snakes and scorpions. He brought you water out of hard rock. He gave you manna to eat in the wilderness, something your ancestors had never known, to humble and test you so that in the end it might go well with you. *You may say to yourself, "My power and the strength of my hands have produced this wealth for me." But remember the LORD your*

God, for it is he who gives you the ability to produce wealth, and so confirms his covenant, which he swore to your ancestors, as it is today. (Deuteronomy 8:10-18)

God was essentially warning Israel about the dangers of success and prosperity. He reminded them not to be prideful because their very ability to create wealth and success came from God, and he warned them never to believe that they could truly prosper apart from God.

I believe that one of the greatest traps that leaders fall into is believing their own press clippings: "I must be great because other people are saying so. And look what I have accomplished." Leadership always comes with power, and power has a way of going to our heads. We feel the affirmation of those who selected us for our leadership position and the esteem of those we now lead. Pride easily takes root in the soil of leadership. And pride begins to disconnect us from God.

ONE OF THE GREATEST TRAPS THAT LEADERS FALL INTO IS BELIEVING THEIR OWN PRESS CLIPPINGS.

A prideful leader becomes arrogant, impressed with their own abilities and giftedness, forgetting that all these things were bestowed on them by God. A prideful leader thinks primarily of their own status and success to the detriment of others. But humble leaders seek the success of the entire team. Prideful leaders listen only to their own counsel, while humble leaders listen to the counsel of many. Prideful leaders see other people as a means to their desired ends, but the humble leader sees the welfare of his or her people as an end unto itself.

We have all seen examples of leaders who are self-centered and full of themselves. Such people are all too common in our workplaces and in the public square. They often act as if the normal rules don't apply to them. They justify their bad behavior based on their own

HUMBLE LEADERS SEEK THE SUCCESS OF THE ENTIRE TEAM.

sense of superiority, and they often leave behind them a wake of destruction. Often, but not always, their arrogant behavior leads to their downfall, but not before great damage has been done to the institution they led and the other people who worked there. And I think I can say with confidence, no one wants to be led by an arrogant, self-important leader.

EASIER SAID THAN DONE

So how does one become a humble leader? How does one avoid the temptations of power, success, and self-importance? Once again, it begins with surrender: "Not my will, Lord, but thy will. How can I better know, love, and serve you in the place you have put me?" As I have said more than once, surrender of our will is a lifelong process, and it requires that we keep our relationship with God fresh each day by spending time in his Word and in prayer.

But there are some practical things we can do as well. As you lead others, give them permission to challenge your thinking and to disagree with you when they believe they have a better idea. Don't allow yourself to become the "emperor without clothes" whom people are afraid to speak truth to. Embrace the fact that God has distributed gifts and talents to all the people on your team, and that if you can release all of their gifts and talents you will make better decisions and accomplish greater things than the leader who embodies a "my way or the highway" attitude.

Taking this approach will require daily reinforcement. It has been my experience that people are always somewhat intimidated by—even fearful of—the boss. They are not likely to take the risk of disagreeing with you unless they feel completely safe in doing so. And the first time you bite their head off for disagreeing with you is the last time they will risk expressing a better idea or a different way. But if they see that their idea actually changed your mind or influenced the outcome of a decision, they will be emboldened to contribute more ideas. I would sometimes start a meeting by stating that I wanted to hear everyone's opinions and that I hoped we could have an open debate about the issues we were going to discuss. I specifically asked people to challenge my ideas and push back when they disagreed. I even told them that they weren't very helpful to me if they wouldn't disagree when they felt I was wrong. You have to work at creating this kind of positive culture on your team. Surround yourself with smart people, give them permission to challenge you, and show them that you value what they have to say. And be sure to give them credit when their contributions have made a difference.

When I became the CEO of Parker Brothers Games, one of the challenges I faced was trying to lead a group of vice presidents who were more than twenty years older than me. It was difficult for me, as I'm sure working for someone so much younger was difficult for them. Within days I could feel the undercurrents of resentment in the ranks. I understood that attempting to command them to respect me wouldn't work, so instead I sought to earn their respect. I spoke about the importance of each member of the leadership team to our success. And I talked about pulling together to face our challenges. I felt like I was making some progress, with the exception of one holdout: Bill, the vice president of sales and a critical member of our team. Bill was in his mid-fifties and had more than thirty years of experience in the toy industry. He knew everyone and was highly and widely regarded. But I could tell from Bill's body language that he did not support my appointment to the presidency.

So, one day I walked into his office, shut the door, and asked if we could talk. I said something like this: "Bill, I can tell that you were not pleased that I was appointed as president. I get it. But you need to know that I did not seek this job and that I also fully understand that I was not ready for it. Nevertheless, I was asked by our parent company to step into this role. I know this much: I cannot succeed, and the company cannot succeed, unless we all come together as a team. I have great respect for you. You are a critical leader here. You have forgotten more about the toy industry than I will ever know. And I most definitely cannot succeed without your wisdom, advice, and support. So I am asking today for your help. Will you give it to me?" Bill paused to consider what I had said, then looked me in the eye and extended his hand to shake mine. "I can work with that," he said. From that day on I had Bill's full support. The price of his support? Showing some humility.

ANOTHER FIRST DAY IN THE CORNER OFFICE

A few years after the executive-toilet episode at Lenox I had another first day in a corner office. This time it was twenty-five hundred miles away at World Vision, near Seattle. After multiple panic attacks over leaving my career behind and nervously following God's call into a job for which I had few qualifications, I found myself coming in early again to my new corner office on my first day. But this time I was in a very different place emotionally. Instead of being puffed up about being the new CEO at World Vision, I was terrified. I was overwhelmed with the responsibility of leading an organization on which millions of children depended for life itself. I felt totally unprepared to lead a team of people who knew far more about global poverty than I did. I had no experience with these issues. I had been selling fine china to the wealthy just a few days earlier, for heaven's sake. In short, I felt completely helpless and inadequate.

And so, that morning I sat at my desk and literally cried out to God. "Lord, it took every ounce of courage I have just to show up here today. I have no idea what to do or how to lead in this place. I am unqualified and unprepared for what lies ahead. Help me, Lord, please help me!" I was kind of pitiful, literally whimpering to God from my new corner office. And that's when I came about as close as I ever had to hearing God's voice. This is what I heard: "Rich, I have you exactly where I want you, helpless and totally dependent on me. I have worked for twenty-five years to bring you to this place of total surrender. You have been obedient, and now I want you to trust me and watch what I will do. I've got this, Rich." And I realized at that moment the truth of Paul's dialogue with God about weakness: "But he said to me, 'My grace is sufficient for you, for my power is made perfect in weakness.' Therefore, I will boast all the more gladly about my weaknesses, so that Christ's power may rest on me" (2 Corinthians 12:9). You see, God isn't impressed with our strength; he wants us humbled and totally dependent on him in our weakness. Only then do we have full access to God's power working through us. "For all those who exalt themselves will be humbled, and those who humble themselves will be exalted" (Luke 14:11).

9

INTEGRITY

WHO YOU ARE WHEN NO ONE IS WATCHING

SCRIPTURE ➤

"Who may worship in your sanctuary, LORD?
   Who may enter your presence on your holy hill?
Those who lead blameless lives and do what is right,
   speaking the truth from sincere hearts.
Those who refuse to gossip
   or harm their neighbors
   or speak evil of their friends.
Those who despise flagrant sinners,
   and honor the faithful followers of the LORD,
   and keep their promises even when it hurts.
Those who lend money without charging interest,
   and who cannot be bribed to lie about the innocent.
Such people will stand firm forever." (Psalm 15:1-5 NLT)

LEADERSHIP PRINCIPLE ➤ Integrity is one of the most powerful values a leader can possess and the bedrock of a leader's credibility. It creates a cascade of positive outcomes for a team or an organization, including trust, unity, motivation, and improved morale and productivity.

It's more important to do the right thing than to do things right.

PETER DRUCKER

Consistency OF Strength & Reliability

Iᴛ ʜᴀs ʙᴇᴇɴ sᴀɪᴅ ᴛʜᴀᴛ INTEGRITY is doing the right thing, even when no one is watching. In other words, a leader's private behavior is a good indicator of their true nature. If their private behavior is honest and ethical, it is likely that their public behavior can be trusted as well. This has always been one of the litmus tests for integrity because it speaks to the consistency of one's character. And here is a universal truth: everyone appreciates and values coworkers and bosses who demonstrate integrity. And these are the same people employers want to hire and promote because of the positive impact they have in the workplace.

A LEADER'S PRIVATE BEHAVIOR IS A GOOD INDICATOR OF THEIR TRUE NATURE.

But integrity of this kind in the workplace is sadly not the norm.

→ Story about FedEx → Boss said people look to me for leadership.

THE "CLINT TEST"

Early in my career I was put to the test on this principle of private versus public behavior in one of my first job interviews. I was twenty-five years old at the time and had a full day of interviews set up for that entry-level marketing position at Parker Brothers Games. I was impressed that even for an entry-level job they had arranged for me to meet with several vice presidents, three marketing directors, and even a "drive by" with the president. I really wanted this job, so I did my best to make a positive impression. Then at lunch I was kind of surprised that they sent me out for almost two hours with a much lower-level employee named Clint, who worked as a marketing research analyst. I doubted that his input would matter much compared to the directors and vice presidents. But off we went to a local eatery.

As I recall, Clint and I had a good time eating fried clams somewhere in Salem, Massachusetts, and talking about what it was really like to work at Parker Brothers. A few days later I was thrilled to get the call that they were offering me the job. When I showed up for my first day of work a couple of weeks later, I spent the morning with my new boss getting briefed. But his opening comments are the ones I remember to this day. (I seem to have a lot of important first days on the job.) He looked at me and said: "You know why we hired you, don't you?" Of course, I'm thinking it must have been my scintillating interview technique, my winning personality, my prematurely graying hair, my impressive Wharton MBA, or maybe my solid twenty months of previous work experience. But no, he said, "You passed the 'Clint test.' We knew you would be on your best behavior with the directors and the VPs, but we wanted to see if you were a jerk when your guard was down, so we sent you out to lunch with Clint. You passed. Clint told us he thought you were a good guy, so we hired you." Wow! And I thought no one was looking. Forty-three years later, Clint and I still exchange Christmas cards every year.

Since integrity is such a broad concept, let me break it down into three categories: personal, relational, and corporate.

PERSONAL INTEGRITY

I believe that integrity is the North Star of leadership. It is the moral and ethical compass that allows a leader to navigate any and every situation with the confidence that they are traveling in the right direction. Without such a North Star, leaders can easily lose their way in the storms and rough seas of life and work. Without integrity, leaders are adrift in relativism and expediency, making it easy to wander far from the plumb line of uncompromising ethics.

A leader with integrity provides her staff with the confidence that she will always strive to do the right thing, the fair thing, no matter what. She keeps her word and treats people with respect. People trust a leader like that and always know where they stand. That helps the whole organization to work with confidence and to focus on achieving the mission. Integrity may be the single most important quality a leader can possess. I think of it as kind of a superquality, because when a leader consistently demonstrates integrity it results in a cascade of positive outcomes. A culture of trust is built, fear and anxiety diminish, employee morale and even customer satisfaction improve, and productivity increases. And doesn't everyone want to serve under a leader who consistently demonstrates personal and moral integrity?

In contrast, a leader with little or no integrity creates a cascade of negativity in the workplace—fear, suspicion, self-dealing, defensiveness, confusion, discouragement, and toxic office politics. Yet the beauty of this superquality is that integrity does not require skill, education, intellect, or vision. Integrity is about character and trustworthiness, and it is accessible to everyone on the organization chart from the receptionist to the CEO.

INTEGRITY IS ABOUT CHARACTER AND TRUSTWORTHINESS.

→ Jesse Leaving the Church

However, I also need to note that it's also possible that integrity could disadvantage you in certain situations. You may work in an environment in which you feel pressured to bend the truth, do unethical things, or go along with the crowd in doing something wrong. Not every workplace plays by ethical rules. In a situation like this, behaving with integrity could come with a cost.

I was once actually fired for my values. I worked for a person who led by wielding fear, anger, abuse, and shame to drive performance. She created a dark and oppressive work culture that wounded people.

As much as I could, I sought to shine a little light in that darkness by being a voice of integrity, fairness, and encouragement—trying to protect my team from her abuses whenever I could. I tried to hold on to my values rather than capitulate to hers. The day she fired me, she told me that it was not performance related; it was because I made her feel uncomfortable because she knew that I "didn't approve of her methods." Because she was "uncomfortable," I was out of work for the next nine months. So, yes, sometimes there is a price to pay when we try to live out our faith at work. But Jesus never promised us a faith that costs us nothing.

RELATIONAL INTEGRITY

When we think of a lack of integrity, we tend to think first about lying, stealing, or cheating. These are the "poster child" illustrations of behaviors that lack integrity. But integrity is a much broader concept than that. The whole area of relational integrity influences all our interactions with others. Have you ever used words and phrases like these to describe people in your workplace, church, or community: hypocrite, phony, egotist, out for themselves, two-faced, double-dealing, opportunist, self-serving, poser, back-stabber, kiss-up, slippery, shady? I didn't realize how many of these monikers we had created until I started to list them. Every one of these descriptors speaks to the issue of relational integrity. What do other people see in us when they interact with us? Integrity in our relationships requires that we deal with others honestly, sincerely, transparently, considerately, and fairly. People should feel safe with us, knowing that we will never try to use them to our advantage, that they can trust us, count on us, and confide in us.

Why is this so important? Think about what happens in an organization where relational integrity is lacking. Someone says something about you behind your back, so you decide you'll find a way to get even. Someone else says something that embarrasses you in a meeting, so you avoid that person because you find them unpleasant. Then you are rude to a person who comes asking for your help, and now they start avoiding you, and so on and so on. Before you know it, the organization becomes toxic and crippled. People are shambling through the halls like Jacob Marley's ghost, dragging behind them the heavy, clanking chains of fractured and dysfunctional relationships. Dan can't work with Mark. Susan tries to avoid Ashley. Dave can't be trusted. Heather is ruthlessly ambitious. Everyone is gossiping about what a jerk Frank is. Does this sound familiar? ↗ the Kisser

Don't be that person! Don't keep score and hold grudges. Keep short accounts and forgive people who treat you poorly. Be the one who is a breath of fresh air, the person everyone trusts, the one who is working for the greater good. It has been my experience that most bosses want people like that on their team, and every organization wants to hire people who add that kind of value. In the short term, acting with that kind of integrity might sometimes hinder your career, but in the long term, integrity usually proves to be a winning attribute.

I once worked with an executive coach who gave me a good piece of advice that I've never forgotten. He told me to embrace a simple four-word question in the workplace: How can I help? When your phone rings, answer by saying, "Hi, this is Rich, how can I help?" If someone walks into your office, look up and say, "Hi, how can I help?" He said that if I approached people with that helping spirit, I would find that everyone would want to work with me. I would become more useful and valuable to the organization. And while I haven't literally taken his advice word for word, I have tried to make that spirit of helpfulness the hallmark of my leadership approach.

Now, for a Christian, integrity should mean much more than just some management technique that can be used for tactical advantage. Moral and ethical principles must derive from some standard of truth and rightness that doesn't change from year to year or situation to situation. In fact, most ethical behavior that we take for granted today derives from the Judeo-Christian ethic. Fairness, justice, honesty, kindness, generosity—they're all biblical principles that have shaped our Western culture for thousands of years. Integrity is foundational to our Christian faith and a requirement of our commitment to God that we will live our lives according to his teachings. If we are to be effective ambassadors for Christ in our workplaces—our one job—we must be people of integrity. Paul speaks of the importance of doing the right thing, not just because God is pleased, but because other people are watching us. This verse was printed on all our paystubs at World Vision: "For we are taking pains to do what is right, not only in the eyes of the Lord but also in the eyes of man" (2 Corinthians 8:21).

CORPORATE INTEGRITY

Integrity is not just a quality that individuals can possess; it can also characterize the culture of an entire organization. And the culture of an organization is usually defined by its leaders. Huge organizations can develop cultures in which deception, greed, abuse, and expediency result in disastrous outcomes. In recent years we have seen appalling behavior by drug companies promoting opioids knowing full well how addictive they were. Wells Fargo set up those thousands of bogus bank accounts in people's names without their knowledge to drive profits. Fox News fostered a toxic culture of sexual misconduct that ultimately toppled its CEO and other prominent on-air personalities. Theranos, the Silicon Valley medical start-up, turned out to be a colossal hoax. Its founder created a culture of deception and fear to conceal the fact that its blood-testing technology didn't actually work. The list of such scandals is long, but they all have a common root cause: the lack of integrity and adherence to moral, ethical principles and honesty. Behind every one of these scandals is the failure of leadership in an organization to define values, establish expectations, and set positive examples through their own words and actions.

At World Vision we often spoke of "tone at the top," asking what kind of example we as leaders were setting for everyone else. Were we collaborating well, respecting one another, adhering to ethical standards, and speaking with positive and inspiring words? Were we committed to the mission of the organization and willing to make sacrifices for the greater good? And were we living out the values we wanted to characterize World Vision?

PUMPKIN SEED INTEGRITY

Early in my tenure at World Vision I had an opportunity to lift up integrity as a core organizational value after discovering that one of our marketing programs had been compromised. Once a year World Vision would send out a mass mailing to almost two million people trying to attract new donors to the organization. The most effective of these mailings included an attention-getting device. In an appeal for donations to help African farmers, we included in the envelope a packet of real pumpkin seeds, stating that if the person sent those seeds back to us with a contribution, we in turn would send the seeds to a farmer in Africa, who would then receive agricultural training from World Vision, enabling them to grow pumpkins and other crops to feed their family. Something about that offer was very compelling, and every year thousands of good-hearted people responded. It was one of our most successful campaigns—until I discovered one day that there were thousands of packets of pumpkin seeds piling up in our warehouse. Apparently, people had mailed them back to us as we had asked, but this year, instead of sending them to the farmers, as we had done in the past, they had been accumulating in our warehouse. We had used the cash gifts people had sent to help the farmers as we had promised, but we had not sent the actual pumpkin seed packets.

When I investigated further, I discovered that a couple of people in our marketing department felt that sending the actual pumpkin seeds to Africa was inefficient and didn't make economic sense, so that year they had decided not to send them. I was glad to know that only a couple of junior staff members had been involved with this decision. They were right that sending the actual seed packets was somewhat inefficient, but that wasn't the point. Their decision had breached our integrity, and we had broken a promise to our donors. When I found this out, I was angry. As a charity, the single most important asset we owned was our integrity. Thousands of people sent us millions of dollars each year because they trusted us. They believed that we would do what we promised. Lose that, and we could lose everything. In a tense meeting with the CEO (me), I let these individuals know that I would not tolerate any breach of integrity with our donors no matter how insignificant it might seem. And I insisted that they now work with the warehouse to send those seeds to the farmers as we had promised.

Then I called an all-staff meeting to present the results of our investigation and use it as a teachable moment. I said something like this: "All of us work hard here to grow our revenue every year so that we can help more people. And I know that all of you feel the pressure to achieve that growth. But I want you to hear this loud and clear. No matter how much pressure you are under to grow revenue— integrity *always* trumps revenue. The ends never justify the means if the means require us to do something deceptive with our donors. Let me be clear. You will probably not lose your jobs here if you miss your revenue goals, but I can promise you that if you compromise our integrity, you will not continue to work here. Is everyone clear on this now?"

I think that was about as harsh as I ever got as a leader. That incident, I was told by staff members later, brought both clarity and relief to the organization. The leader was saying he valued integrity more than results. It was okay to miss a target from time to time, but it was never okay to do something unethical. It clarified and reinforced the culture of integrity at World Vision. In fact, I think that incident led to establishing an "integrity hotline," making it easy for employees to anonymously report any ethical violations they saw right up to the board of directors.

There are entire books about the importance of integrity, and it is hard to do it justice in one short chapter. But hopefully you now see its importance for everyone, but especially for leaders. One of the verses in the New Testament that I often inscribe when someone wants me to sign one of my books is Matthew 5:16 (CEV): "Make your light shine, so that others will see the good that you do and will praise your Father in heaven." We have the privilege of reflecting the light of Christ in our workplaces and communities. We have the opportunity to shine our lights in places that are sometimes dark, to be a presence of calm in the midst of storms, and to be a voice of reason in stressful situations. That is the power of integrity. And when we live out the Great Commandment to love our neighbors, by loving and caring about our coworkers, we draw people to the light of the gospel because they see something different in us, something attractive, compelling, and life-giving. We show them a different way to live and work together by bringing the kingdom of God to work with us every day.

10

VISION

SEEING A BETTER TOMORROW

SCRIPTURE ➤ "Now when Jesus saw the crowds, he went up on a mountainside and sat down. His disciples came to him, and he began to teach them. He said:

'Blessed are the poor in spirit,
   for theirs is the kingdom of heaven.
Blessed are those who mourn,
   for they will be comforted.
Blessed are the meek,
   for they will inherit the earth.
Blessed are those who hunger and thirst for righteousness,
   for they will be filled.
Blessed are the merciful,
   for they will be shown mercy.
Blessed are the pure in heart,
   for they will see God.
Blessed are the peacemakers,
   for they will be called children of God.
Blessed are those who are persecuted because of righteousness,
   for theirs is the kingdom of heaven.'" (Matthew 5:1-10)

LEADERSHIP PRINCIPLE ➤ One of the chief tasks of a leader is to create a vision for a different and better future, and a belief that it can be achieved.

Vision without action is merely a dream. Action without vision just passes the time. Vision with action can change the world.

JOEL A. BARKER

Good leaders must communicate vision clearly, creatively, and continually. However, the vision doesn't come alive until the leader models it.

JOHN C. MAXWELL

VISION, OR VISION CASTING, may be one of the most difficult leadership qualities to embody because it calls on a leader to envision the future. A leader has the responsibility to chart the course, provide direction, and set priorities for the group or organization they are leading in order to arrive at some desired future state. But seeing the future is not easy. I have compared this task to driving a bus at night on a winding road in a snowstorm at seventy miles an hour with no headlights or windshield wipers while all of the passengers are complaining about your driving skills.

Leading with vision is hard. Nevertheless, providing a compelling vision for any organization or endeavor is a crucial element for creating clarity, unity, and motivation. When a team has an understanding of where they are now, where they need to go, and what it will take to get there, it provides the clarity they need to pull together to achieve the task.

Since vision casting can seem like some mysterious kind of divination, I find it helpful to break the process down into four parts. A leader must define the current reality, articulate a desired future, identify a way forward, and personally "own" the vision. Let me speak to each of these four elements and provide some examples.

DEFINING REALITY

Before a leader can envision a desired future, they first need to have a thorough understanding of the present. In other words, before you set a destination it's helpful to know where you're starting from. This is why your GPS asks for your current location before it sets the course to your destination. What I have found over many years of experience is that organizations often have a distorted view of reality. They are often blinded by assumptions about their situation that are incorrect. Jim Collins talks about confronting "the brutal facts of reality" as an essential step for leaders. Albert Humphrey's SWOT analysis (strengths, weaknesses, opportunities, threats) is an exercise designed to help organizations clearly define the reality of their current position. Failure to understand the present reality affecting an organization can have disastrous results. The American auto companies foolishly dismissed the threat of Japanese imports, believing that Americans would never switch to Japanese cars. Kodak failed to adapt to the digital revolution, blinded by the profitability of their film business. When I worked at Parker Brothers Games, management had a hard time seeing that video games would become a threat to conventional board games. I championed the notion that we were not in the board-game business but rather the home-entertainment business, and two years after our video-game launch we had doubled the size of our one-

A VISION FOR A BETTER FUTURE BEGINS WITH A SOBER ASSESSMENT OF THE CURRENT REALITY.

hundred-year-old company. You get the idea. A vision for a better future begins with a sober assessment of the current reality.

Let me use a case study from my time at Lenox China. When I was made president over the fine china division, I knew about as much as you do about the fine china market—in other words, almost nothing. And to make it worse, the Lenox leadership team also knew that I knew nothing, which made it a bit challenging for them to have confidence in their new leader. So I confessed to them that I knew nothing (there's that humility thing) and asked if they would help me by providing a thorough orientation to the industry. I knew that I couldn't be an effective leader unless I first developed my own "worldview" about Lenox and the industry in which it competed. In short form, here is what I learned over those first weeks and months:

> After more than fifty years as number one, Lenox had lost its top market share position to Noritake, an import from Japan.

> Lenox designs had gotten progressively more sophisticated and more expensive, especially compared to Noritake, who had less expensive and simpler designs. Lenox's last few new product-line introductions had flopped.

> Lenox executives looked down their nose at Noritake and other competitors because they considered them cheap, inferior, and inelegant imports. (Does this sound a little like the auto industry in the 1970s?)

> The core customer for fine china was a twenty-four-year-old bride and her mother, since weddings were when most couples acquired their tableware.

There was a lot more to it than just these four points, but you get the gist. I realized that I had to help the Lenox leadership team see the reality of their current situation before I could help them chart a course toward a better future. And this process of defining reality, getting the facts on the table, was just as important for them as it was for me.

ARTICULATING A DESIRED FUTURE

In this particular case, articulating a desired future was pretty easy. The team at Lenox desperately wanted to regain its number-one share position. We had lost credibility with our department-store buyers. We were losing shelf space to other brands more attuned to the bridal customer. And our factories were struggling because of declining volumes. And so we set the goal of becoming number one again by taking seriously our lower-priced competitors and also listening more carefully to our core consumers' needs and desires.

IDENTIFYING THE WAY FORWARD

Next, we had to set a course to achieve this. As the leader, I took a few key steps that would reinforce the reality of our situation. First, I set up a "war room" in the conference room where we had all our team meetings. I asked that place settings of the top fifty bestselling china patterns in the market be displayed on shelves in descending order in that room. I wanted the team to see every single day what the most successful and bestselling china patterns looked like. And while they mocked many of the patterns for being naive and simplistic, I just kept telling them that, like them or not, these were the products young brides were buying. I persisted in the process of defining reality.

Next, I told them that we were going to take every new Lenox design and show it to several hundred brides and their mothers before launching. Only the new patterns that received high marks from our target customers would go to market. At this the designers all rolled their eyes because, of course, they knew better. They were the designers and they had art degrees. The brides almost always seemed to select patterns with simpler, more versatile designs over the very elaborate and sophisticated ones. I argued that our challenge was to design patterns that were elegant, simple, and affordable. And we agreed to only introduce new patterns that passed the "bride test" first. We also talked with department-store buyers to gain their market insights and worked with our factories on strategies to lower our costs to be more competitive. We had a lot of work to do.

OWNING THE VISION

It's not enough for a leader just to define reality and help determine a way forward; he or she must totally own the vision of a better future. A new vision doesn't become a reality because the leader sends it out in an email to everyone. The leader needs to visibly embody the vision—to eat, sleep, and drink the new vision—day in and day out in full view of the organization. Changing deeply held beliefs and entrenched behaviors is hard. A whole industry has grown up around change management, helping organizations to socialize and internalize the sweeping changes needed for them to succeed. And the best leaders lead by example.

In my Lenox example, I was trying to refute the established wisdom that marketers and designers had developed over decades of prior successes. I knew it would not be easy for them to abandon the status quo without some serious efforts. So I took visible steps to own the vision personally.

First, I invested my time and energy in the new vision. Over the next months we held every single marketing and design meeting in that "war room," often referring to what was really selling out there in department stores. We were united around the goal of regaining our number-one position in the market. We rededicated ourselves to putting the customer first. At every trade show I visited every one of our competitors' showrooms so that I could continue my education and get a first look at all their new products. This required hours and hours of traipsing around acres of fine china showrooms. Can you say "torture"? I also committed to sitting in on every new-product design meeting with my team. This was unexpected of the CEO, who typically would delegate those meetings to the marketing and design teams. But I told the team that nothing was more important to the future of Lenox than selecting the new products we would bring to market. So I committed to investing a big chunk of my time there. I owned the vision, preached it every day, and invested my time and energy to make it a reality.

Next, I took a risk and put some skin in the game. I asked them to humor me by having our factory produce four prototype dinner plate designs: one with a narrow band of black with gold around the edge, one with blue and gold, one with green and gold, and one with red and gold. Eyes rolled again. Now the new guy with zero design experience was designing china patterns by himself. But in the process of defining reality for myself, I had become convinced that the simplest ideas, which could also be sold at lower price points, had been overlooked by my designers with art-school training, who were paid to create marvelous new and often expensive designs. Those four simple patterns were also shown to brides in our marketing research, and every one of them scored high marks. And so at the next tableware show we introduced them, rolling eyes and all.

So, what happened? The first of the new patterns that came out of our research and design process started to take off in retail stores. Brides were responding to them, and department-store buyers were ecstatic at the resurgence of Lenox. We were starting to create a buzz in the industry again. Those four simple patterns at lower price points that I had "designed" surprised everyone—even me. Out of more than seven hundred active china patterns in the market, one of them hit the top ten, two more hit the top twenty, and the fourth made the top fifty. Brides loved their simplicity and their price.

Our goal of becoming number one again and our strategy for getting there had turned the skeptics into believers and ultimately united the whole company around this shared vision. And, of course, there is nothing better than success to unite a team and get them excited about the future, not to mention some nice bonus checks.

Over the next several years, Lenox's market share went from 26 percent to 45 percent, while Noritake's share fell by more than ten points. The Lenox comeback started with *defining reality* and facing the hard facts. Out of that the *vision* of becoming the industry leader again emerged. That, in turn, helped us to identify a *way forward* involving many targeted steps and a lot of hard work. Finally, I as the leader had to roll up my sleeves and *own the vision*. I had to invest my time and energy working side by side with the other members of the team. I had to believe in it if I expected them to believe in it.

Okay, this example from Lenox probably doesn't sound like it belongs in a book about the spiritual qualities of a leader. But if you accept my earlier premise that God uses leaders to change the world by shaping and redeeming human institutions, then the methods for accomplishing that are also spiritually important. Proverbs states, "Where there is no vision, the people perish" (Proverbs 29:18 KJV). Casting a compelling vision for a desired future not only helps corporations to thrive; it can also improve the effectiveness of churches, Christian ministries, our school systems, our communities, and our government as well.

THE VISION OF JESUS

I want to close this chapter by pointing you to the example of Jesus, whose compelling vision of a different way for men and women to be in relationship with God changed our world. Jesus was the master of vision casting. These were very first words he uttered after being baptized by John: "The time has come. The kingdom of God has come near. Repent and believe the good news!" (Mark 1:15). He announced that God's kingdom was now finally coming, that it was good news, and that all people needed to do to enter this new kingdom was to repent and believe. Then he spent the next three years preaching his vision of the coming kingdom.

Think about what he accomplished during those three years. He not only transformed the prevailing paradigm of the centuries-old Jewish faith; he replaced it with a radical new vision of the kingdom of God. His captivating new vision launched a revolution that motivated and empowered that first generation of Christians in remarkable ways. Despite persecution, martyrdom, opposition from the Jews, and the iron fist of the Roman Empire, this new faith movement multiplied and spread. By the fourth century, Christianity had become the official religion of the Roman Empire. In the centuries since it has profoundly changed and shaped every dimension of our human existence: law, justice, human rights, government, business, education, marriage, family, and charity, to list just a few. And two thousand years later, the Christian faith has more than two billion adherents. That was the power of the way Jesus shaped a new vision for human flourishing during his three short years of public ministry.

So how did he do it? He used the same four principles I outlined above. He defined the current reality for first-century Jews, offered a fresh and compelling vision of a better future, revealed a new way forward in the relationship between God and humanity, and totally owned and modeled this new vision of a different future.

Jesus had a daunting change-management task. Let's look at the Jewish faith in first-century Palestine—the context in which Jesus lived. Judaism had come to be dominated by the corrupt and legalistic leadership of the Pharisees and Sadducees. They had worked out a power-sharing arrangement with Rome, which protected their leadership status over the Jewish people. They wielded that power and control in ways that created a rigid class system, which placed them at the top while pushing the poor, the uneducated, and even the sick and the lame to the bottom. They ran the temple system in ways that extracted money from the poor in order to sustain their own power and authority. Jesus knew he needed to call out their hypocrisy in order to establish his own vision for God's chosen people. The old paradigm had to be discredited and replaced with the new.

Now if you study the four Gospel accounts, there were just two intense moments when Jesus expressed fierce anger and outrage. The first was when he angrily lectured the Pharisees, calling them "hypocrites," "blind guides," "a brood of vipers," "whitewashed tombs," and "children of hell" (see Matthew 23). He did not mince his words. The second moment came when he expelled the money changers from the temple by ransacking their tables and stalls shouting that they had turned what was meant to be a house of prayer into a den of robbers.

In both examples, Jesus was visibly challenging the current reality in which God's chosen people were living. He was putting the brutal facts on the table and upending the status quo by revealing just how far the Jewish people had wandered from God's heart and intent for them. Jesus was defining reality for the Jewish people by revealing the corruption of their leaders.

But Jesus also had to articulate a more desirable future and clarify a different way forward. He had to replace the old paradigm with a new one. If the status quo was unacceptable, what was the better future that God wanted his people to see and embrace? Jesus laid out this new vision with remarkable clarity and poignancy throughout the Gospel accounts, but perhaps nowhere more forcefully than in the Sermon on the Mount. Whole books have been written on this passage from Matthew, but let me just highlight a few of the elements that underscore how Jesus used this teaching to replace the old paradigms with a fresh new vision for God's chosen people.

He started with the Beatitudes: blessed are the poor in spirit, the meek, the merciful, the pure in heart, those who mourn, those who hunger and thirst for righteousness, those who are persecuted, and the peacemakers. It's hard for us to grasp how radical these pronouncements were to Jews living in the Roman Empire under the leadership of the Pharisees and Sadducees. Jesus was essentially saying that all the people who had been persecuted, exploited, and excluded were now loved, valued, and included. The "down and outs" were now "up and in"; they were the ones considered blessed by God. Jesus was casting a vision for a new reality by turning the prevailing social hierarchy upside down.

Next, he established his legitimacy: "Do not think that I have come to abolish the Law or the Prophets; I have not come to abolish them but to fulfill them" (Matthew 5:17). Jesus was reassuring the crowd by saying that, yes, the Law and the Prophets were from God and that he had not come to invalidate them but instead to fulfill them. This was messianic language. It was a kind of a dog whistle that signaled that he might just be the prophesied Messiah of God who would finally liberate the people.

And then, after reciting the beatitudes, Jesus fired off a riff that completely reinterpreted and reapplied the law as it pertained to murder, adultery, divorce, oaths, vengeance, and love of neighbor. This amounted to a radical new understanding of God's law applied to the human heart. In each case he used these specific words: "You have heard that it was said . . . but I tell you . . ." For example, Jesus said: "You have heard that it was said, 'Love your neighbor and hate your enemy.' But I tell you, love your enemies and pray for those who persecute you, that you may be children of your Father in heaven" (Matthew 5:43-45). Do you see how Jesus was replacing the perfunctory legalism of the Pharisees with a deeper call for people to think and act differently by examining the motives of their hearts? This was what God desired from his people, not some check-the-box, mechanical obedience. It was a new way forward, a way to internalize the commandments they had been taught. Again, it's hard for us to imagine how revolutionary this teaching would have been to his first-century audiences.

And then, after the six consecutive "reboots" of these venerable commands of the law, he then goes on to redefine giving, prayer, fasting, worry, materialism, and the practice of judging others. Finally, he warns the people to beware of false teachers and then ends with the story of the wise and foolish builders as a way of summarizing everything he has just taught them.

In one hundred and seven verses containing about two thousand words, Jesus laid out his radically new vision for ethics, morality, and the relationship between God and humanity. He had illuminated a new way of living in obedience to God and in harmony with God's intent. Of course, later on, through his death and resurrection, he opened the way for that relationship to be fully restored through the forgiveness of sins.

So how did the people gathered there respond to this new possibility? "When Jesus had finished saying these things, the crowds were amazed at his teaching, because he taught as one who had authority, and not as their teachers of the law" (Matthew 7:28-29). Jesus had effectively shown the people a better and more hopeful future and provided the teaching to help them realize it.

Jesus owned this vision with a total commitment. In encounter after encounter Jesus modeled these new teachings. He healed the sick, restored sight to the blind, lifted up the brokenhearted, and reached out to those beyond the established circle of Jewish life. He demonstrated in his life the values he espoused: inclusion, compassion, kindness, generosity, truthfulness, integrity, humility, prayer, and forgiveness. He spoke in parables that reinforced and amplified these values. And he never compromised his vision. Finally, Jesus made the ultimate sacrifice to lead his followers back into right relationship with God by going to the cross so that sins might be forgiven once and for all time. Jesus provided the ultimate example of a leader lifting the eyes of his people to see a new and better vision and to embrace a new reality. Jesus was even willing to die for them.

And that brings me to another critical quality for a godly leader: courage.

COURAGE

DO NOT BE AFRAID

SCRIPTURE ➤ "Be strong and courageous. Do not be afraid; do not be discouraged, for the LORD your God will be with you wherever you go." (Joshua 1:9)

LEADERSHIP PRINCIPLE ➤ Leaders who demonstrate courage when facing tough challenges and decisions will inspire their teams to overcome their own fears, enabling better performance and greater focus on desired outcomes.

---

*I learned that courage was not the absence of fear,
but the triumph over it. The brave man is not he who
does not feel afraid, but he who conquers that fear.*

NELSON MANDELA

BEING A LEADER IS HARD. In some ways, it is so much easier to be a follower, leaving the tough decisions to somebody else. That way your decisions never get criticized, you never have to risk being wrong, and you won't get the blame when a decision turns out badly. Risk, blame, and criticism come with leadership. They just do.

It has been said that courage is the opposite of fear, but I disagree. Fear is something we all feel, while courage is the determination to overcome our fears. As Chae Richardson put it, "Courage is not living without fear. Courage is being scared to death and doing the right thing anyway." If we lead with a moral compass directing us, that North Star of integrity I spoke of in an earlier chapter, we will inevitably face situations where doing the right thing will come at a cost. It will require courage.

In chapter ten I spoke of the process of leading an organization into a desired future state by casting a compelling vision. But leading into the future, which is always unknown, often creates fear—fear of change, fear of taking the wrong course, fear of what might happen. And overcoming those fears requires courage on the part of the leader. Even though the leader may share some of those same fears, he or she must be able to manage them in a way that instills confidence in the rest of the team. Billy Graham once said, "Courage is contagious. When a brave man takes a stand, the spines of others are often stiffened."

FEAR OF A DOOMSDAY VIRUS

On my first overseas trip as the new president of World Vision, I came face to face with the AIDS pandemic. And what I saw made me afraid. I saw it first in the lives of three orphaned boys who were living alone in their mud hut because both of their parents had died from AIDS. For a guy who had been selling fine china to the wealthy sixty days earlier and had never been to Africa, it was both shocking and gut-wrenching. AIDS was a terrifying disease that stealthily crept from village to village in much of sub-Saharan Africa, killing men and women in their prime and leaving millions of children orphaned. If you were infected, it was almost 100 hundred percent fatal. I later described it as a "doomsday virus," the kind of thing that is the stuff of apocalyptic disaster movies. The global breakout of coronavirus in 2020 has given America and other developed countries a better idea of the fear and the suffering that Africa experienced during the peak of the AIDS crisis.

And yet in the late 1990s, back home in America, no one seemed to be talking about AIDS in Africa or even seemed to be aware of what was happening. And to some extent, that included my colleagues at World Vision. You see, AIDS was deeply stigmatized and politicized back then. Christians perceived it as the direct result of immorality, and some even felt that the disease was God's punishment on people who had committed sexual sins. Few understood how it was devastating Africa, as husbands spread it to their wives, and mothers to their children through childbirth.

I returned from that trip determined that World Vision needed to tackle this AIDS issue and find a way to bring help. We needed to help those infected, the orphaned children left behind, and the grandmothers who were now caring for their grandchildren. And to do this, World Vision would have to raise a lot of money from our child sponsors and donors. But first we would have to overcome our own fears.

When I convened a meeting and laid out my intentions to our leadership team, I could feel the uneasiness in the room. Instead of being met with a chorus of enthusiasm, I could see my team looking at each other with fear and discomfort. Their glances told me what they were thinking: "How do we tell the new guy he can't go there?" Finally, the vice president of marketing spoke up and said: "Rich, World Vision is a G-rated ministry, and this is an R-rated issue. Our donors and church partners will never support this. It's too controversial. And if we 'go there,' it could really damage our reputation." There, he had said it.

I don't remember the entirety of the discussion that day but, after listening to the various points of view in the room, I made a decision. At the end of our meeting I said something like this: "You are right that this will be a controversial issue and an uphill battle. But I believe that many of our donors and church partners are wrong about this. We need to educate them about what this disease is doing to people in Africa, especially the children. Once they know the truth, I believe their minds will change and they will get behind us. And if we don't show them that they are wrong about this, who will? God has given us a front-row seat to the human suffering AIDS is causing—and God help us if we fail to speak up. This is our 'Esther moment,' and I believe God will withdraw his hand of blessing from World Vision if we fail to do the right thing at such a time as this. So yes, we're 'going there.'"

I agreed that we would first do some marketing research to test the issue with the Christian public to see how much resistance we were likely to encounter, and the results were even worse than we had anticipated. We asked a large sample of evangelical Christians this question: "Would you be willing to donate money to a reputable Christian organization in order to help children orphaned by AIDS?" This seemed to me to be a no-brainer—of course they would help the children. But then we got the results: just 3 percent of evangelicals said they would definitely be willing to help; 52 percent said they probably or definitely *would not* help!

The reaction of Christians to the AIDS issue, even when speaking only of innocent children, was far more visceral than we had imagined. Virtually every other demographic we surveyed, including non-Christians, showed a greater willingness to help. We had our work cut out for us. But by now my team was starting to rally around the cause. It was not the expedient thing for World Vision to do, but it was the right thing. And for the next few years, we put our response to the AIDS pandemic in the center of our strategic bull's-eye. *In teresting to note that ALL Sin has brought Sickness into the WORLD*

A CAMPAIGN CALLED HOPE

We named our new campaign the Hope Initiative and launched it at our annual major-donor conference in New York City, knowing that we first needed to convince our biggest supporters of the legitimacy of our cause. Rather than focusing on those who had contracted HIV, we instead focused on helping "orphans and widows in their distress," a direct quote from James 1:27. We knew that we could find more sympathy for the widows and children left behind than for the men who had spread the virus. We emphasized both care for these widows and orphans but also AIDS prevention by teaching abstinence and faithfulness to one's spouse. We partnered deeply with African pastors and churches, as we saw them as critical to the solution. We brought in pastors from Africa and even children who had been orphaned by AIDS to tell their stories in the first person at our donor conference.

Next, we launched a new kind of child sponsorship, called Hope Child, specifically to support orphans and vulnerable children impacted by AIDS. And we began an eighteen-city tour in which we took our message to people and churches across the United States— preaching, holding donor events, and speaking to the media to raise awareness. It's not an exaggeration to say that our AIDS response and our challenge to American Christians consumed World Vision for much of the next five years.

We did face strong criticism from some Christian leaders and organizations who labeled us as "liberals" and publicly opposed our efforts. Some wanted nothing to do with this because it involved helping people who had committed sexual sins. We had to face some strong headwinds. Nevertheless, we remained resolute in our determination to demonstrate the love of Christ to communities that had been ravaged by this disease.

While this is not the place to tell the full story of World Vision's response, the bottom-line outcome is that we did succeed in turning the tide of public (Christian) opinion around this issue. Of course, we were not the only voices advocating on this issue. Other organizations and leaders spoke out as well. Many of our partner churches embraced the cause and sent delegations to Africa to see, learn, and help. Hundreds of thousands of Hope children were sponsored, and hundreds of millions of dollars were raised. We even helped influence Congress to pass, on a bilateral vote, President Bush's PEPFAR initiative (President's Emergency Plan for AIDS Relief), the largest single foreign assistance program since the Marshall Plan, which helped rebuild Europe after World War II.

After five exhausting years of campaigning, World Vision had played a significant role in changing the attitude of Christians toward AIDS and had helped millions of men, women, and children across Africa. Not only did it not damage our reputation, it enhanced it. Increasingly our supporters saw us as the organization that would take on the toughest challenges in order to help the most desperate people on the planet.

But it had started with fear: fear of alienating donors and partners, fear of damaging our reputation, fear of facing AIDS itself, fear of failure, and even fear of what others would say about us. And to overcome that fear, it took courage.

YOU WANT ME TO DO WHAT?

For the Christian the opposite of fear is not courage but faith. If we believe that we are doing the right thing, if we believe that we are doing something close to the heart of God, then we can count on God's support. We can trust God for the outcome. Our faith leads to trust, and trust enables courage. There are many remarkable stories of courage flowing out of faith in Scripture.

Moses offers a great example of both fear and courage. God called on Moses to approach the most powerful man in the world, Pharaoh, and demand that he release all his Israelite slaves, totaling several hundred thousand men, women, and children. To Moses it sounded like a suicide mission. And for several chapters in Exodus we read a remarkable conversation between God and Moses. Moses is having none of it. He snivels and whines and offers excuse after excuse as he tries to convince God that he has the wrong man. Moses is afraid. God, on the other hand, reasons with Moses and promises that he will go with him and protect him. After many verses of dialogue, the conversation culminates with these verses:

> Moses said to the LORD, "Pardon your servant, Lord. I have never been eloquent, neither in the past nor since you have spoken to your servant. I am slow of speech and tongue."
>
> The LORD said to him, "Who gave human beings their mouths? Who makes them deaf or mute? Who gives them sight or makes them blind? Is it not I, the LORD? Now go; I will help you speak and will teach you what to say."
>
> But Moses said, "Pardon your servant, Lord. Please send someone else." Then the LORD's anger burned against Moses. (Exodus 4:10-14)

FOR THE CHRISTIAN THE OPPOSITE OF FEAR IS NOT COURAGE BUT FAITH.

"Please send someone else to do it." Have you ever dreaded doing something that much? I think all of us can relate to Moses' fear. God is asking him to do something that sounds insane. It will take some amazing courage to do the things that God is asking. But God is trying to tell Moses that he needs faith, not courage; faith that God will go with him, protect him, and deliver the outcome. He's simply asking Moses to trust him. And, of course, we know that Moses finally, if reluctantly, overcomes his fear, obeys God, and becomes one of the greatest heroes of the Old Testament. But it started with fear—raw, terrifying fear. Ultimately, it was his faith that overcame his fear and produced the courage he needed. God could be trusted.

Forty years later, after he had led the Israelites through the desert to the brink of the Promised Land, Moses died, and Joshua was installed by God as the next leader for his people—the one who would finally lead them into the land God had promised. Joshua had the difficult task of both replacing the great Moses and leading the military operation required to secure the land. It was another moment where fear had to be real. So God has an important conversation with Joshua just as he had with Moses so many years earlier:

> After the death of Moses, the servant of the LORD, the LORD said to Joshua son of Nun, Moses' aide: "Moses my servant is dead. Now then, you and all these people, get ready to cross the Jordan River into the land I am about to give to them—to the Israelites. *I will give you every place where you set your foot, as I promised Moses.* Your territory will extend from the desert to Lebanon, and from the great river, the Euphrates—all the Hittite country—to the Mediterranean Sea in the west. No one will be able to stand against you all the days of your life. *As I was with Moses, so I will be with you; I will never leave you nor forsake you. Be strong and courageous,* because you will lead these people to inherit the land I swore to their ancestors to give them." (Joshua 1:1-6)

He ends his "pep talk" with Joshua by restating his promise: "Have I not commanded you? *Be strong and courageous.* Do not be afraid; do not be discouraged, *for the LORD your God will be with you wherever you go*" (Joshua 1:9).

Can you see how God reasons with Joshua just as he had with Moses? He promises that he will be with Joshua—that he will never leave or forsake him—and then tells him to "be strong and courageous." In other words, if Joshua has faith in God's promises, it will enable his courage. Faith enables courage.

In the course of my career I have experienced fear more than a few times: fear of making a big decision, fear of changing jobs, fear of losing my job, fear of what other people think of me, fear of doing the wrong thing, fear of failure, fear of success. And those are just some of the job-related fears I have had. The list gets longer when I add things such as health, finances, marriage, kids, and family. Fear is a common human emotion. But our faith enables us to put our fear in perspective.

> **OUR FAITH ENABLES US TO PUT OUR FEAR IN PERSPECTIVE.**

PERSPECTIVE IS EVERYTHING

Have you ever recorded a sporting event involving your favorite team or player and then watched the recording after the game was over? If you already know that your team has won, it's amazing how calmly and objectively you can watch the game with that perspective. But if you don't know who won, every single play is anxiety producing and nerve wracking.

As Christians, we know how the game ends, and we know that our team wins. Yes, in our lives there will be setbacks and bad plays and maybe some injuries along the way. We may even find ourselves two touchdowns behind in the first quarter, but we have the bigger picture; we know the final score. We just need to have faith and trust in God. Remember, "Courage is not living without fear. Courage is being scared to death and doing the right thing anyway." We need to just keep doing the right thing, no matter the consequences, and then trust God for the outcome. That's courage. Faith produces trust, and trust enables courage. God's got our back.

Just before Jesus went to the cross, he spoke to his disciples to prepare them and to encourage them. He knew the persecution and hardship they would have to face after he left them. His words to them should also encourage us. "Peace I leave with you; my peace I give you. I do not give to you as the world gives. Do not let your hearts be troubled and do not be afraid" (John 14:27). "I have told you these things, so that in me you may have peace. In this world you will have trouble. But take heart! I have overcome the world" (John 16:33).

12

GENEROSITY (GREEDLESSNESS)

THE TOXICITY OF MONEY

SCRIPTURE ➤ "Those who want to get rich fall into temptation and a trap and into many foolish and harmful desires that plunge people into ruin and destruction. For the love of money is a root of all kinds of evil. Some people, eager for money, have wandered from the faith and pierced themselves with many griefs. But you, man of God, flee from all this, and pursue righteousness, godliness, faith, love, endurance and gentleness." (1 Timothy 6:9-11)

LEADERSHIP PRINCIPLE ➤ Money and the pursuit of money can be corrosive. Leaders who treat money as a means to an end rather than an end in itself can lift the eyes of their team to the higher purpose of their work.

Money is a terrible master but an excellent servant.

P. T. BARNUM

When we start being too impressed by the results of our work, we slowly come to the erroneous conviction that life is one large scoreboard, where someone is listing the points to measure our worth. And before we are fully aware of it, we have sold our soul to the many grade-givers.

HENRI NOUWEN

LET'S TALK MONEY. It is simply impossible to talk about leadership without discussing the profound influence of money on leaders, the people they manage, and the institutions they lead. The love of money, or greed, can be a cancer in our lives and in the places we work. I wanted to name this leadership quality "greedlessness," but since that is not a word, I chose "generosity" as the leadership virtue that stands in opposition to greed, because a leader characterized by generosity is a person who sees money as a tool, not as an idol.

Dealing with money in our personal and work lives is unavoidable. We all need a certain amount of money in order to provide basic things for our lives and our families. Corporations, schools, governments, and nonprofits need to focus on financial outcomes in order to measure their performance and satisfy their constituents. In this sense, money serves as one of the key vital signs that our families and our employers are in good health—kind of like our heartbeat and blood pressure do for our physical health. Scripture is correct in stating that money itself is not the problem but rather the love of money. It is our relationship to money that has the potential to be so damaging to our lives and the lives of those around us if we are not careful.

My wife, Reneé, has always had a healthy relationship with money. For most of my career she had no idea how much money I earned because it just wasn't important to her. More than a few times in our marriage she has rescued me from my own propensity to let money cloud my judgment. Once, while I was at Lenox, I had been offered a higher-paying job by another employer and I was agonizing over whether to take it. When I discussed it with Reneé, she helped put the decision in perspective for me: "Money is a lousy reason for doing anything," she said. "What would you do if you took the money out of the equation? Which job will you like better? Which company would you rather work for? How will you feel about leaving your work colleagues and relationships behind?" And, of course, "Have you prayed about this to seek God's will in the matter?" After I looked at it from that perspective, I turned the higher-paying job down.

When my daughter Grace was once considering a job change, I shared this perspective on money with her, and she rightly pointed out that only people who have enough money can say, "Money is a lousy reason for doing anything." For many people, money must be a factor in their decision making because of the pressing financial realities of their lives. If you can't pay your rent and feed your family, you must of course consider financial issues in your decision making. With a pretty steep rent to pay in New York, Grace took the higher-paying job. Still, the principle holds: money shouldn't be the sole consideration.

Years after I turned down that higher-paying job offer, when Reneé and I were discussing whether I should give up my corporate career to join World Vision, I brought up the shocker that it would mean a 75 percent pay cut. We had five kids to put through college, so I thought that this reality might even cause her to pause and consider the financial ramifications. Her response? You got it: "Money is a lousy reason to do anything." Then she added, "We need to be where God wants us to be and trust him to take care of us. If this is where God is calling us, then we need to go." World Vision, here we come! And, over all the years of our marriage, Reneé has always been the one to urge us to give more of our money away to worthy causes and people in need. For her, money is just a tool that can be used to do good, and she has always trusted that God would provide for us if we were faithful with our money. This is what a healthy relationship with money looks like in our personal lives. But what about our work lives?

WHEN MONEY BECOMES TOXIC

The pursuit of money can have all kinds of unintended consequences where we work. The almost-universal human quest for more money and greater wealth infects virtually every organization on the planet. The love of money, like the drive for success, is like that carbon monoxide leak in your home: you can't see it, smell it, or taste it, but it can poison you if you're not careful.

Stop and think for a moment about the pervasive influence of money in your place of work. All of us are paid with money. Money is used as a proxy for your worth as an employee, with more "valuable" employees being paid more than less valuable employees. Incentive systems almost always involve money. Perform well and you will get more of it; perform poorly and you will get less. Money creates jealousies and inequities in our workplaces, and those paid less often resent those who are paid more. Money can be like gasoline on the fire of office politics as it motivates some people to posture and maneuver so that they are in the best position to get more money than their coworkers. Money provokes some people to lie or misrepresent their results. Money can also motivate theft, embezzlement, or even just cheating on expense reports. And, if that's not enough, money is the motive for a huge percentage of all crimes committed in the world. Money is a necessary but dangerous thing that must be handled with care.

MONEY IS A NECESSARY BUT DANGEROUS THING THAT MUST BE HANDLED WITH CARE.

Again, while money is an essential tool, it is also a "drug" with a lot of adverse side effects.

But perhaps more damaging than all the above is that *money sometimes replaces purpose* in an organization. Let me say that again: money sometimes replaces purpose. Steve Jobs, the cofounder of Apple, said this about money: "Apple's goal isn't to make money. Our goal is to design and develop and bring to market good products. . . . We trust as a consequence of that, people will like them, and as another consequence, we'll make some money. But we're really clear about what our goals are."

Isn't it interesting that the creator of one of the most successful companies in history said that their goal was not to make money? Steve Jobs understood that money is no substitute for purpose. Apple became a great company because he focused on its higher purpose to design and develop remarkable products. Money can become a counterfeit purpose that infiltrates an organization and over time replaces its higher purpose. At first, it may be unnoticeable, and the company can continue to perform well. But over time, if a higher purpose isn't lifted up by its leaders, the company just becomes a host organism for people who want to extract money from it. And the people who work there become just pawns on the gameboard, the means to the end of bigger salaries and bonuses for the executives and shareholders. Taken to the extreme, organizations like this can become a threat to society.

Sadly, there are far too many examples of companies that put money and profit ahead of the greater good. Consider again those drug companies that sold and promoted opioid-based medications for pain relief. What started out as a positive and even noble purpose—to help people manage their medical pain—ultimately became a national addiction crisis, as greedy executives pushed to promote and sell more pills even when they knew that widespread and uncontrolled access to these drugs was leading to addiction and even death for tens of thousands of customers. Money had replaced purpose, and the results were devastating.

The best organizations lift the eyes of their employees and shareholders to their higher purpose and meaning. As I mentioned earlier, one thing I noticed right away when I moved from the for-profit world to World Vision was the different cultural norm around money. When I worked at Lenox, money factored into everything. As with most corporations, there were elaborate bonus programs based on a variety of performance indicators, and there were stock-option programs for top executives. The higher you were on the organizational chart, the bigger your bonus could be as a percentage of your base salary. Getting a bonus and maximizing your bonus became an obsession. And, predictably, in addition to motivating some of the right behaviors, it also motivated many of the wrong behaviors.

THE BEST ORGANIZATIONS LIFT THE EYES OF THEIR EMPLOYEES AND SHAREHOLDERS TO THEIR HIGHER PURPOSE AND MEANING.

One of the things I tried to do to mitigate this money culture at Lenox was to refocus the organization on its core values and higher purpose. We worked for months on creating a mission statement that would give our employees a greater sense of pride in what they did. Now you might wonder how the mission statement of a hundred-year-old fine china and crystal company could be inspiring. But here's what we came up with: "Enriching people's lives through beautifully designed and crafted products." You see, we weren't just selling dishes, we were enriching lives. Lenox products played a role in weddings, birthdays, and anniversaries, and in Christmas, Easter, and Thanksgiving dinners. Our products were present in the most meaningful occasions in people's lives. And lifting our employees' sights to this higher purpose gave them a renewed sense of pride in the company. And like Apple, if we got our employees focused on making "beautifully designed and crafted products," people would buy them, and we would all make some money. But money wasn't our purpose.

I found a completely different culture at World Vision. As a nonprofit Christian ministry, there were no bonuses, and people worked for a lot less money than they could have made elsewhere. In fact, the higher you were on the organization chart, the bigger the discount your salary got from your market value. The top executives were making 50 to 75 percent less than they could have made in the for-profit world. It was like working in a place that spoke a different language. But what was amazing about this non-money-obsessed culture was that people were there because they believed in the cause—that higher purpose I mentioned earlier. The mission of helping the poor in the name of Christ was incredibly motivating. More than once I had VPs ask me *not to give them a raise* because they didn't want one! Yes, you read that correctly. I remember negotiating with a candidate for the CFO job at World Vision who said he would only accept the job if I paid him no salary! I said that I had to pay him a salary but that he could do with it as he pleased. He then asked if I would pay him the lowest possible salary for his grade level. I hired him and I believe he has donated that salary (and more) back to the organization every year he has worked there.

When I wrote my first book, *The Hole in Our Gospel*, I realized that I would be paid royalties on every book sold. I had several kids in college then, and the extra money would have been helpful. But I struggled with the notion of making money by writing a book about the plight of the poor. I also felt that it would be a conflict of interest because World Vision intended to promote the book with our donors and church partners as a ministry tool. It didn't seem right that I, as the leader, should profit from that. So I made the decision that all royalties from the book should go directly to the work of World Vision. The publisher actually had trouble writing the contract because they had never had an author refuse royalties before. Over the next few years several million dollars of royalty payments went to World Vision's ministry.

But you say, "That's a Christian ministry, and people work there to serve God." Well, here's the thing: the place you work is your place of Christian ministry, and you have also been placed there to serve God. So these same principles apply to you: money is not your purpose for being there; ministry is. Your "one job" is to be an ambassador for Christ in the place you live and work, and you need to be careful not to allow your personal pursuit of money replace that God-given purpose. For the Christian leader, having the right perspective on money is critical.

YOU CAN'T SERVE TWO MASTERS

So what does Scripture have to say about all of this? A lot. Consider these statistics:

> ➤ Sixteen of Jesus' thirty-eight parables deal with money

> ➤ There are 2,350 verses about money and possessions in the Bible, compared to just 500 about faith and prayer

> ➤ One out of every seven verses in the Gospels deals with money

You get the idea. God considers our relationship to money to be of critical importance.

Jesus said: "No one can serve two masters. Either you will hate the one and love the other, or you will be devoted to the one and despise the other. You cannot serve both God and money" (Matthew 6:24). He speaks of the inevitable struggle between these two possible masters. It's a warning. The allure of money and material wealth can become so powerful that it will compete with God for primacy in our lives. Insidiously, our ambition for more wealth becomes our master as it crowds out God's purposes for our lives and replaces God as the source of our security and identity. Paul explains the danger of money even more explicitly:

> Those who want to get rich fall into temptation and a trap and into many foolish and harmful desires that plunge people into ruin and destruction. For the love of money is a root of all kinds of evil. Some people, eager for money, have wandered from the faith and pierced themselves with many griefs.
>
> But you, man of God, flee from all this, and pursue righteousness, godliness, faith, love, endurance and gentleness. (1 Timothy 6:9-11)

Notice that the *desire for wealth,* not wealth itself, is the temptation that leads to a trap, which can plunge us into "ruin and destruction," lead us away from our faith in God, and "pierce us" with "many griefs." So many of the biblical passages about money are like flashing red letters that spell out the word *warning!* And what does Paul suggest that Timothy do to avoid this trap? "Flee from all this, and pursue righteousness, godliness, faith, love, endurance and gentleness." Paul urges Timothy to run from this love of money and instead pursue Christlike values—in other words, a godly character. If we buy into the lie that money is the way we keep score in the game of life, then the true purpose of our lives and our work will be replaced by the need to make more and more money. We cannot serve both masters.

As a leader in your workplace you have an opportunity to be a person who is not "owned" by money. You can put the well-being of people ahead of money. You can focus your efforts and those of your team on higher values such as excellence, in-

MONEY IS YOUR SERVANT, NOT YOUR MASTER.

tegrity, perseverance, and diligence, and create a workplace that allows people to flourish as they focus on the mission of the organization, not just their compensation. Show them that money is your servant, not your master. Because money is a lousy reason for doing anything.

13

FORGIVENESS

I'M SORRY

Mark & mike (handwritten)

↓ (handwritten arrow)

Even When we Didn't Know we hurt Someone. (handwritten)

SCRIPTURE ➤ "Be kind and compassionate to one another, forgiving each other, just as in Christ God forgave you." (Ephesians 4:32)

"If we claim to be without sin, we deceive ourselves and the truth is not in us." (1 John 1:8)

LEADERSHIP PRINCIPLE ➤ Apology and forgiveness heal broken relationships and promote organizational health. Leaders need to model forgiveness in the workplace both by offering it and asking for it.

> *Forgiveness is not an occasional act, it is a constant attitude.*
>
> **MARTIN LUTHER KING JR.**

Forgiveness is central to the christian story. Sin rears its ugly head for the first time early in Genesis when Adam and Eve disobey God in the Garden. And since that moment, the drama of human history has been a tragic blizzard of deceit, selfishness, greed, violence, racism, exploitation, poverty, and injustice.

Fortunately, there is also a great deal of goodness, decency, and compassion to be found in our world. However, while *sin* may sound like an obsolete word in today's world, it is at the heart of broken relationships and all forms of human dysfunction, including those in the places where we work and serve. But all of Scripture tells the story of the lengths to which God has gone to offer his forgiveness to us, ultimately through the death and resurrection of his Son, Jesus Christ. Our God is like the father in Luke 15, waiting to forgive and welcome home his prodigal son who had betrayed him and squandered his inheritance.

At the core of our faith is the knowledge that we are broken people, incapable of restoring our relationship with God, or with each other, through our own efforts alone. And that admission of our own brokenness is foundational to understanding and navigating our relationship with God and with those around us—including those in our workplaces. → David's Greatess Streongth was

Our vertical relationship with God can only be restored when we repent of our sins and accept God's forgiveness, made possible through Christ's atoning death. The process goes like this: *sin* ➤ *repentance* ➤ *forgiveness* ➤ *restoration*. Through repentance and forgiveness, that which was broken becomes whole again. It is restored. God's model of forgiveness and restoration can also transform the horizontal relationships we have with family, friends, spouses, coworkers, and even enemies. These human relationships always manifest some degree of brokenness due to our sinful nature.

In a marriage, for example, repentance and forgiveness are crucial to maintaining a healthy and loving relationship. Inevitably when two people are living together in close quarters, there will be friction, conflict, and hurt feelings. Without regular repentance and forgiveness, scar tissue can build up until the relationship is in crisis, much in the same way that cholesterol building up in our arteries will lead to a health crisis. The two most powerful words in a marriage relationship are, "I'm sorry." When we admit to and repent of our hurtful words or actions, we can clear the air and restore health and balance to the marriage. We must learn to forgive others as Christ forgives us.

FORGIVENESS AT WORK

In the same way, leaders must conduct themselves with the knowledge that they too, are broken and flawed people, both needing forgiveness and willing to forgive others. But it has been my observation that the whole concept of repentance and forgiveness is rarely invoked in our places of work. And yet, as in a marriage, during the normal course of human interaction in a workplace, people say and do hurtful things, and they make mistakes that affect those around them. But those simple and powerful words, "I'm sorry," are rarely uttered. And they are spoken even more rarely by leaders, perhaps because apology and forgiveness require leaders to be vulnerable and acknowledge their faults, something many are uncomfortable doing.

As I mentioned in chapter nine, the cumulative effect of careless words and office sleights can become crippling to an organization, as each member of the team nurses their own anger and pain resulting from the careless (or intentional) hurtful words and actions of others. As in a marriage, relational "cholesterol" builds up and becomes harmful to our organizational health.

We cannot control the ways others conduct themselves in our workplaces, but we can control our response to their actions. And that often means forgiving people who never apologize for their words or their behavior. When we intentionally choose not to hold grudges, we help reduce that bad cholesterol that can so easily clog our work relationships. And by doing this we prevent small resentments from escalating into major conflicts.

Jesus spoke to this very issue: "But to you who are listening I say: Love your enemies, do good to those who hate you, bless those who curse you, pray for those who mistreat you. If someone slaps you on one cheek, turn to them the other also. If someone takes your coat, do not withhold your shirt from them. Give to everyone who asks you, and if anyone takes what belongs to you, do not demand it back. Do to others as you would have them do to you" (Luke 6:27-31). This sets a high standard for the way we are to respond to those who provoke us, and yet a leader can set the example of repentance and forgiveness for others to model. Let's say that as a leader you scolded someone in anger in a public meeting. Pulling that person aside later and apologizing can be healing and restorative. It also makes you less likely to do the same thing again. Even more powerful is when a leader apologizes for a mistake or a harsh word in a more public setting. A leader's willingness to apologize and also to forgive others can be a powerful tool in creating a healthy culture.

I once received an email from a lower-level employee who was so upset by a decision I had made that he demanded my resignation—not the smartest move, to demand that the boss resign. My first instinct was to lash back at him for his audacity. Instead, I waited a few weeks to cool down and then approached him with an unexpected gesture, apologizing for the way in which my decision had impacted him. It was a way of showing him that I understood why he felt hurt. We had a long, healing conversation and became even closer colleagues afterwards. People deeply appreciate a vulnerable leader who is willing to admit their mistakes and own them with integrity. And it helps create a culture where everyone becomes accountable for their occasional mistakes or bad behavior.

LEADERS MAKE MISTAKES

Leaders are entrusted with power, and with that power they make decisions that impact their organizations and the people in them. When a leader makes a mistake or a bad decision, it can have consequences that are far-reaching. That is why it is critical for leaders to be willing not only to recognize their mistakes but also to apologize for them and take steps to repair the damage they have caused. A leader who won't take responsibility in this way can have a devastating effect on an organization and the people who work there. Conversely, a humble leader who recognizes their mistakes, owns them, and course-corrects will earn the respect of their team and create a healthy culture in which authenticity, forgiveness, and restoration are normative.

> **IT IS CRITICAL FOR LEADERS TO BE WILLING NOT ONLY TO RECOGNIZE THEIR MISTAKES BUT ALSO TO APOLOGIZE FOR THEM.**

Sadly, in today's world we too often see well-known leaders who are caught abusing their power and doing scandalous things. Some are exposed in a moral failure; others are found lying, misappropriating funds, harassing staff, or unethically using their power for personal gain. But think of how rare it is for those who are caught to offer a sincere, remorseful apology. Apologies often have the sense of "I'm sorry I got caught," rather than the more authentic, "I'm truly sorry because what I did was wrong." And when such a leader refuses to own their bad behavior, accept the consequences, and sincerely ask for forgiveness, they can never realize the kind of restoration that is available to them from both God and from the people they have harmed.

One of the greatest leaders in the Bible, King David, was described as a leader "after God's own heart." But like all leaders, David made mistakes, sinned against God, and made decisions that had consequences for the people he led. In one of David's greatest failings, his power, pride, and ego caused him to sin against God when he instructed his subordinates to conduct a head count of his vast armies, an exercise in pride and vanity that took almost ten months to complete. The story is told in both 1 Chronicles 21 and 2 Samuel 24.

> Satan rose up against Israel and incited David to take a census of Israel. So David said to Joab and the commanders of the troops, "Go and count the Israelites from Beersheba to Dan. Then report back to me so that I may know how many there are."
>
> But Joab replied, "May the LORD multiply his troops a hundred times over. My lord the king, are they not all my lord's subjects? Why does my lord want to do this? Why should he bring guilt on Israel?"
>
> The king's word, however, overruled Joab. (1 Chronicles 21:1-4)

Notice that Joab, representing the commanders of the troops, had the courage to "speak truth to power" and strongly advised David not to do this. Joab could see that this foolish command was driven by David's pride and that it would unnecessarily anger God and bring guilt on Israel. But despite Joab's respectful but passionate warning, David does it anyway, giving further evidence of his prideful motives. In an earlier chapter I spoke of how important it is for leaders to surround themselves with good people, give them permission to disagree, and to listen to their counsel. David's power and egotism made him unwilling to listen.

After nine months and twenty days of tedious census taking, Joab returned to the king with the results. But now, perhaps after having those many months to think about his actions and his motives, we finally see David realizing his sin, an arrogant reliance on the might of his armies instead of God's power. "David was conscience-stricken after he had counted the fighting men, and he said to the LORD, 'I have sinned greatly in what I have done. Now, LORD, I beg you, take away the guilt of your servant. I have done a very foolish thing'" (2 Samuel 24:10).

Here we see the first step in the process of repentance ➤ forgiveness ➤ restoration. David owns his mistake, recognizes his sin, and begs God to forgive him. He apparently does this in a public way so that all his people witness the admission of his mistake and the sincere repentance of their leader. But nevertheless there are serious consequences of David's error.

> Before David got up the next morning, the word of the LORD had come to Gad the prophet, David's seer: "Go and tell David, 'This is what the LORD says: I am giving you three options. Choose one of them for me to carry out against you.'"
> So Gad went to David and said to him, "Shall there come on you three years of famine in your land? Or three months of fleeing from your enemies while they pursue you? Or three days of plague in your land? Now then, think it over and decide how I should answer the one who sent me." (2 Samuel 24:11-13)

In David's case, the consequences of his actions were given to him by God in the form of three choices. Here we see a chastened leader who still must lead; he still must manage the consequences of his mistake on his people. David is confronted by God with another far-reaching leadership decision. The first two options, famine and war, would be devastating to his people but would likely shield him and his family from any harm due to his wealth and position. The third option, a plague, would mean that he and members of his family would be equally vulnerable to God's punishment. Showing both care for his people and trust in God, David chose option three.

> David said to Gad, "I am in deep distress. Let me fall into the hands of the LORD, for his mercy is very great; but do not let me fall into human hands." So the LORD sent a plague on Israel, . . . and seventy thousand of the people from Dan to Beersheba died. (2 Samuel 24:14-15)

> David said to God, "Was it not I who ordered the fighting men to be counted? I, the shepherd, have sinned and done wrong. These are but sheep. What have they done? LORD my God, let your hand fall on me and my family, but do not let this plague remain on your people." (1 Chronicles 21:17)

After the plague ravages tens of thousands of David's people, a horrified and penitent David begs God to relent, asking that he and his family be allowed to take the punishment instead. Here we see a shepherd leader who now fully understands the disastrous fallout from his mistake on innocent people. He again publicly admits his sin and offers his own life in payment. David's repentance is complete. At this point the Lord stops the plague on the site of the threshing floor of Araunah the Jebusite and commands David to build an altar there, where he will then make a sacrifice for his sin.

The end of this episode is worth exploring. A prideful David has sinned against God. His sin had dire consequences that affected the entire nation. David has repented of his sin publicly and with great anguish and sincerity. Seeing his genuine repentance, God has forgiven David and relented in his punishment. But David still seeks to make restitution before God by building an altar to offer sacrifices on the site where the plague was ended, the threshing floor of Araunah the Jebusite. When Araunah offers the king his property at no charge, David refuses, saying: "No, I insist on paying the full price. I will not take for the LORD what is yours, or sacrifice a burnt offering that costs me nothing" (1 Chronicles 21:24). David understands that he must bear the cost of the land because the forgiveness of his sin comes with a cost. And so David buys the land, builds an altar, and offers sacrifices to God.

LEADERS MUST OWN THEIR MISTAKES

There are some practical principles we can derive from this remarkable story of sin and redemption for leadership today.

First, David let his power and pride go to his head. He was motivated by ego rather than what was best for the people he led. He insisted that his commanders carry out months of hard work with the single goal of making him feel more powerful. This abuse of power is common in modern workplaces when leaders operate out of self-interest rather than prioritizing the greater good.

GOOD LEADERS SHOULD ALWAYS ENCOURAGE HEALTHY DISSENT.

Second, good leaders should always encourage healthy dissent. And while leaders sometimes have to overrule their team members, they should do so only after giving strong consideration for the opposing view, especially if that view is almost unanimous. David didn't listen to the advice of his senior leaders who not only saw his mistake but respectfully and clearly advised him not to do it. He had more than nine months to change his decision as the census continued but stubbornly proceeded.

Third, when a leader finally realizes his mistake, he should own it publicly, apologize with sincerity, and seek the forgiveness of those who have been affected. This is what genuine repentance looks like in a leader, and it is the only thing that can restore respect and confidence in a leader who has made a significant mistake. Denial and blame-passing don't inspire loyalty or confidence.

DENIAL AND BLAME-PASSING DON'T INSPIRE LOYALTY OR CONFIDENCE.

Finally, a leader needs to work to undo the damage that has been done. Even after realizing his catastrophic sin, David still had to steer the nation through the fallout. And when the plague finally ended, he took further steps to demonstrate his remorse by purchasing the land, building an altar, and offering sacrifices.

David was by no means a perfect leader. Even as a leader after God's own heart, he made terrible mistakes and had some horrific moral failings. (Remember his affair with Bathsheba and the murder of her husband?) But because David responded to his own mistakes and bad behavior with integrity and sincere remorse, he is still considered one of the greatest leaders in all of Scripture. David was a true values-driven leader who earned the respect of his people through good times and bad.

As a postscript to David's story, that piece of land he bought from Araunah has a significant symbolic meaning in the story of Scripture. The threshing floor of Araunah was located on Mount Moriah, the place where God commanded Abraham to sacrifice his son Isaac but then relented and provided the lamb to be sacrificed in Isaac's place. This profound moment in Israel's history foreshadowed God's intention to provide the sacrifice of his son, the lamb of God, for the sins of all humankind. Araunah's land is also the place where David's son Solomon would build the magnificent temple, the place where God would dwell with his people and where sacrifices would be made daily for the sins of Israel. And almost one thousand years later, not far from Araunah's threshing floor, Jesus Christ would be crucified as the ultimate sacrifice for our sins. This is the very place where God's plan of sin ➤ repentance ➤ forgiveness ➤ restoration unfolded.

A LEADER NEEDS TO WORK TO UNDO THE DAMAGE THAT HAS BEEN DONE.

SAYING YOU'RE SORRY

David's story resonates deeply with me because I too have made leadership mistakes that required forgiveness. Like David, in one particularly painful instance I was strongly advised by some of my team members not to make a decision that they believed was inconsistent with our organizational values and would cause harm to our reputation. But I went ahead anyway, and my poor decision resulted in a great deal of division and controversy. The decision was reversed within days, but the damage had been done and trust had been broken with many of our partners—and it was my fault.

What happened in the weeks and months after speaks to the power of forgiveness to transform broken relationships. For me, it started with repentance—owning my mistake publicly and with genuine remorse. But as Christians, God also calls us to go to those people we have harmed and seek their forgiveness as well. This is hard work in any relationship because it requires approaching the aggrieved person, being vulnerable, admitting that we were wrong, and taking full responsibility for our actions. And so, starting with my own staff and employees, I reached out to many different partners and constituents individually to offer my apology and to ask for their forgiveness. These were difficult but healing conversations, but there were many who encouraged me along the way, graciously receiving my apology and lifting my spirits. In some cases, these hard conversations laid the groundwork for new friendships and partnerships. Slowly and steadily the process of repentance ➤ apology ➤ forgiveness ➤ restoration began to work as I was able to repair many broken relationships and begin turning the page on a difficult chapter for me and for the organization I led. But this restoration process couldn't have happened without sincere apology and forgiveness.

AN APOLOGY WELL DONE

On April 12, 2018, at a Starbucks in Philadelphia, two African American men were waiting to meet a friend. When they asked to use the restroom, they were told they could not because they had not purchased anything. The manager subsequently asked them to leave the store. When they refused, the police were called and the two men were handcuffed, arrested, and removed from the Starbucks. This incident was caught on video and went viral within minutes of being posted, sparking a national outrage at what was seen as an ugly case of racial profiling and discrimination. Starbucks was besieged with anger and criticism.

Kevin Johnson, Starbucks's CEO at the time, suddenly found himself and his company thrust into a national controversy. There were many ways Starbucks could have responded. The CEO could have blamed the store employees, fired them, and simply stated that they weren't representative of the spirit and culture of Starbucks. He could have blamed the police for overreacting and escalating the situation. But instead, Kevin Johnson took full responsibility. Here are several excerpts from his official statement made several days after the incident.

I want to begin by offering a personal apology to the two gentlemen who were arrested in our store. What happened in the way that incident escalated, and the outcome, was nothing but reprehensible—and I'm sorry. I want to apologize to the community in Philadelphia, and to all my Starbucks partners. This is not who we are, and it's not who we're going to be. We are going to learn from this and we will be better for it. These two gentlemen did not deserve what happened, and we are accountable.

I am accountable. . . .

Now there's been some calls for us to take action on the store manager. I believe that blame is misplaced. In fact, I think the focus of fixing this: I own it. This is a management issue, and I am accountable to ensure we address the policy and the practice and the training that led to this outcome.

Here we see a leader sincerely apologizing, demonstrating genuine remorse, taking personal responsibility for what happened, and promising to address both the harm done and the underlying culture within the company that led to the incident. But Kevin Johnson did more than just make a statement and move on. He flew to Philadelphia and met personally with the two men who had been arrested to apologize to them and to make restitution. He also met with both the Philadelphia mayor and police chief. But Johnson knew that dealing with the root causes of this issue would require more than an apology. So, first, Starbucks changed and clarified a policy issue in a letter to all employees stating: "Any person who enters our spaces, including patios, cafes, and restrooms, regardless of whether they make a purchase, is considered a customer." Then, Johnson made an unprecedented commitment to conduct racial-bias training with all 175,000 of Starbucks's US employees, and on May 29 he actually closed all eight thousand US stores for an afternoon to make good on that commitment.

While the full story would take much longer to tell, this leadership moment illustrates the power of forgiveness in a completely secular context. Kevin Johnson admitted that his employees had made a mistake, took personal responsibility for it as the leader, and made a genuine apology to those impacted. He didn't do it simply by phone and press release, he flew across the country to do it in person. He then took decisive steps to make this a teachable moment for all his employees so that Starbucks might emerge stronger and better on the other side of the crisis. He followed the principles of repentance ▶ apology ▶ forgiveness ▶ restoration, and in doing so, he arguably turned a terrible situation around and even increased respect for the Starbucks brand while winning over many of the company's critics.

Forgiveness is a powerful medicine that works at multiple levels in our lives. It can work in the mundane, day-to-day interactions we have with other people and also in moments of monumental crisis. In many ways, forgiveness is a kind of "wonder drug" that can heal the damage caused by a wide variety of ailments. And a leader who understands the need for forgiveness and the power of apology is a leader others will seek to follow.

14

SELF-AWARENESS

KNOW THYSELF

SCRIPTURE ➤ "Why do you look at the speck of sawdust in your brother's eye and pay no attention to the plank in your own eye?" (Matthew 7:3)

LEADERSHIP PRINCIPLE ➤ The best leaders make efforts to become aware of their own weaknesses and shortcomings and learn to understand the magnified impact their words and actions can have on others.

The greatest of faults is to be conscious of none.

THOMAS CARLYLE

Words can inspire. And words can destroy. Choose yours well.

ROBIN SHARMA

I'M SURE MY WIFE WILL BE SURPRISED TO LEARN that I am writing a chapter on self-awareness. As she has on many occasions, Reneé taught me a valuable lesson about this attribute early in our marriage. I was in my thirties and had just been named the new president of Parker Brothers Games. Let's just say that my sails were filled at that time with quite a bit of my own wind. Reneé was at home with our two small children, managing a busy household. At work I was managing about a thousand employees including six vice presidents. A typical day for me was a blizzard of interactions, conversations, meetings, and the doling out of assignments, as people looked to me for key decisions that would affect the company. I was, as they say, "large and in charge." And at the end of my day I would come home brimming with adrenaline.

One day after work I walked into our house and began to interrogate Reneé about what she had done that day. Had she called the repairman for the washer, made an appointment to get our car serviced, paid the utility bills, and so on? (I know, so bad—so, so bad!) I was in full CEO "combat mode," asking questions and driving for outcomes. Reneé was not amused. But instead of getting angry with me, she took me by the hand and said, "Come with me." She walked me back out the door to our front steps. Then she pointed to the door and said: "Do you see this doorway? When you cross that threshold, you aren't the CEO anymore. I'm your wife, not your employee." She was right; I had been incredibly tone-deaf and insensitive.

My behavior in this silly episode showed a complete lack of self-awareness. I didn't realize that I had brought this "command and control" behavior into my home and into my marriage, nor did I see the hurt I was inflicting by being so insensitive to Reneé's feelings, her daily reality, or the sacrifices she had made in order to stay home and care for our children. This was an important lesson learned, not only about marriage but about life. How do other people perceive us? How might our words and actions impact others in negative ways? Why is it that we don't see ourselves the way that others see us, and how is it that we often don't take into consideration the feelings and perspectives of others?

THE SELF-AWARE LEADER

The best leaders make efforts to become aware of their own weaknesses and shortcomings and learn to understand the magnified impact their words and actions can have on others. That's because the best leaders take the thoughts and feelings of other people into account. A leader who is not self-aware is like a blindfolded child playing pin the tail on the donkey with a very sharp tack—dangerous! Self-awareness is complex; it's a multifaceted concept. So let me unpack it in three different dimensions: role awareness, personal awareness, and relational awareness.

THE BEST LEADERS MAKE EFFORTS TO BECOME AWARE OF THEIR OWN WEAKNESSES.

Role awareness is about understanding your unique role as a leader. A leader's primary responsibility is to unleash the full potential of the people on their team in order to accomplish the team's mission and goals. Unfortunately, too many leaders get this backward, instead using their people to advance their own selfish agendas. They use the other members of the team to serve their own interests, make them look good, and help them gain personal advantage— because it's all about them. If you've ever worked for someone like this, you know how demoralizing it can be.

But as I stated in chapter one, a great leader understands that he or she is only one member of a larger team that requires the efforts and talents of all its members to flourish. The conductor of an orchestra is not necessarily the most gifted person—or even the most important—on the stage. They are just the one who has the specific role of leadership. They are there to facilitate and enable the talented musicians to play the music at the highest level they can achieve. Self-awareness for a leader begins with a grounded understanding of their rightful role.

SELF-AWARENESS FOR A LEADER BEGINS WITH A GROUNDED UNDERSTANDING OF THEIR RIGHTFUL ROLE.

Personal awareness is a knowledge of one's own strengths and weaknesses, talents, and deficiencies. What are you gifted at? What are your positive traits? What are your deficits and negative tendencies? Yes, every leader has deficits and negative traits, and a failure to recognize them can be disastrous. As a leader you want to lean into your strengths and talents while taking steps to minimize the impact of your weaknesses and deficiencies. To use a card-game metaphor, we are all dealt a hand of cards in life. We may have a few face cards and a strong hand in one or two suits, but we have also been dealt some twos and threes and may be weak in some particular areas. If a leader is blind to their weaker suits their leadership can be permanently hobbled.

In my own career, I always excelled in the creative side of the businesses I worked in. I loved developing new products and concepts, creative strategies, and advertising. And I was good at those things. But I had little interest or skill in the details of financial management, information technology systems, and manufacturing—things that were critical to our success. I was also not very detail-oriented, so I always needed people to help me manage and keep track of important processes and details.

By understanding my own profile, I could both lean into my strengths and make sure I had others on my team who had strengths in areas where I was weaker. When a leader recognizes their personal soft spots, they also affirm the importance of the gifts and skillsets that others on their team bring to the table. And by understanding and addressing your assets and liabilities you can optimize your whole team's performance. No one wants to work for a leader who thinks they're brilliant at everything because that attitude denigrates the contributions of everyone else.

Relational awareness is about understanding how others see us. When my wife had to remind me that I was not the CEO when I crossed over the threshold of our home, I had been unaware of how my words and behavior were being perceived by her. Being relationally aware means thinking intentionally about how others perceive you—how your words, attitudes, and actions are received by others.

I am a big believer in 360-degree reviews, where a leader is confidentially evaluated by a group of their coworkers. If structured correctly, this tool gives a leader a candid glimpse into exactly how they are being perceived by others. At World Vision, even though I was the CEO, my board insisted that I be subject to a 360 every year. They would ask my direct reports what they thought of my leadership across multiple dimensions and then present the results to me. This always felt a bit uncomfortable because I, like most of us, don't like to hear criticism. And for a few years the board even included my wife in the review because they wanted to know how my work was affecting our marriage and family. Even more uncomfortable! But I've always believed that it is better to know how one is perceived by others than to be ignorant of it.

Once during my time at Lenox, I did 360s on all my direct reports and then sat down with each one of them to review the results. One leader received consistently negative feedback several years running.

While he was gifted and getting positive business results, his staff said he was arrogant, verbally abusive, and intimidating. They said he constantly micromanaged them—telling them how they should do their jobs—and never praised them when they did something well. This was contributing to low morale and even high turnover in his department. Each time I would point to this behavior in his review, he would express shock. "That's not who I am. I am not abusive, and I don't micromanage my staff. And my results speak for themselves." I would tell him that I expected him to be more aware of these issues and to work toward improvement. But after a couple of years of the same criticisms, I became frustrated at his lack of self-awareness. I finally gave an ultimatum: "Look, you may not see these tendencies in your behavior, but this is how others are perceiving you. I believe that *perception is reality,* so either change the perception or change the reality. Either way, you need to address this." Rather than listening to the 360 feedback with an open mind and a spirit of humility, he chose denial instead. A few months later I suggested that it was time for him to move on, and he left the company.

PERCEPTION VERSUS REALITY

Perception versus reality is a tricky concept. We often say and do things with one intent, but the other person hears it differently than we intend. When I was questioning my wife about what she had accomplished during the day, I did not intend it to be hurtful or insulting. I was trying to find out where things stood. I was just seeking information. But my words and my manner came across as accusatory and judgmental. If I had put myself in her shoes for a moment, pausing to consider how my questions might be received after a long, demanding day with a couple of toddlers, I could have avoided the hurt feelings and misunderstanding. What if I had picked up that fussy toddler and taken her upstairs for a story and a bath? What if I had asked how I could help lighten Reneé's load? That would have totally changed the dynamic and her response. But it would have required me to be more attuned to her reality and less concerned about my own. In other words, it required greater self-awareness.

THE POWER DYNAMIC

In a workplace, the perception-versus-reality problem can become magnified by power, position, and money. The people under a leader's authority are keenly aware that their leader has the power and authority to promote, demote, or fire them. Their livelihoods and the well-being of their families depend on staying in the good graces of their boss. The stakes are high. So, in addition to generating some interesting (and usually dysfunctional) office politics, this power imbalance has a way of distorting and magnifying the words that come from a leader's mouth, often with unintended consequences. The "whisper" of the leader can sound like a deafening shout to someone under their authority—and the "shout" of a leader can be traumatizing.

If you say something in anger to a lower-level coworker in a group meeting, or make a flippant comment about them to others, you might forget you said it five minutes later. But those words might devastate that person's self-esteem and confidence for weeks while diminishing them in the eyes of their colleagues. And while that may not have been your intention at all, that was the real negative consequence your words had. Conversely, when you, as a leader, use words to affirm, compliment, and inspire your team members, the positive impact is also magnified—building their confidence, self-esteem, and satisfaction with their work. Self-aware leaders learn to understand the magnified impact of their actions and words.

YOU'RE PROBABLY BIASED

While I won't be able to adequately cover this topic here, a crucial component of self-awareness for a leader is the recognition that gender and racial stereotypes can profoundly and detrimentally distort workplace dynamics. All of us see the world through our unique lens, influenced by our age, race, gender, culture, economic background, and upbringing. Male leaders in particular are often unaware of their own gender biases, not to mention the additional challenges female colleagues may have to deal with that they don't or the privileges that they may have enjoyed throughout their careers without even noticing them. Older leaders will often be blind to the unique challenges faced by Millennials and Gen Z employees. White leaders will tend to underestimate the obstacles faced by team members of color. Gender and racial biases are so deeply ingrained that most people don't even realize that they have them. Women and minorities in particular must struggle against deeply rooted prejudices, often invisible to their co-workers, to gain respect and status as equals.

In my class of MBA students at Wharton back in the 1970s, there were only about twenty-five women—and even fewer minorities—out of some five hundred students. But in the Wharton MBA class of 2021, 47 percent are female and 36 percent are people of color. Things have changed. A similar shift has occurred in almost every academic and professional field over the past few decades. However, while this sea change in our universities and workplaces is less than fifty years old, the biases affecting women and minorities in our culture have been deeply rooted for hundreds of years. And they don't change overnight.

As a white, male, Boomer leader, I realize you may not be that interested in what I have to say about privilege and inequality. But I also realize that as such, I have a responsibility to educate myself, elevate the different perspectives around me, and make a proactive effort to engage with these topics. As my career progressed and I became increasingly aware of my own biases and privileges, I began to listen more intentionally to the voices of female and minority team members and to seek to understand their real frustrations. Whether you are male or female, older or younger, white or nonwhite, it is likely that you also have biases that you are unaware of, and I encourage you to engage in constructive dialogue with team members who are different from you to better understand their unique points of view. If you want to become more self-aware, seek to understand and listen. It will help you unleash the full potential of the gifted people in your care.

IF YOU WANT TO BECOME MORE SELF-AWARE, SEEK TO UNDERSTAND AND LISTEN.

EVERY NATION, TRIBE, AND TONGUE

World Vision, with some forty thousand staff from one hundred countries, is a cauldron of diversity: age, gender, racial, tribal, ethnic, national, and denominational. It gave me a graduate-level course on the marvelous diversity of God's people. World Vision made a deep and conscious commitment to pursuing diversity, equality, and inclusion. As the organization grew out of its white-missionary-sending model of the 1950s and 1960s, it made an intentional commitment to shift toward indigenous leadership, elevating national staff to positions of authority in their home countries. That meant that Ugandans would run World Vision Uganda, Brazilians would run World Vision Brazil, and so on. In subsequent years World Vision also made a determined effort to advance women to higher positions of authority, even in patriarchal societies where this went against the cultural norms. At one point, four of World Vision's seven regional VPs were women—two in Africa, one in the Middle East, and one in Latin America. These changes corresponded with explosive growth that catapulted World Vision to become one of the largest humanitarian organizations in the world. Diversity was also valued on both the global and the many country-level boards. The board of directors I answered to was wonderfully diverse both racially and by gender. I served under four board chairs during my twenty years—two were men and two were women.

My World Vision experiences helped to both reveal and begin to remove my own subtle biases. I recall my first World Vision international trip to Uganda in 1998, just a few weeks after I had started working there. I was introduced to a woman who ran our microfinance program in a rural area of Uganda. She was a gracious Ugandan woman with an infectious smile, but I remember doubting whether she was really qualified to run such a large microfinance program. I am ashamed even now to admit it, but her casual dress and informal manner—and if I am honest with myself, her race and nationality—didn't square with my preconceptions of a "capable financial executive." So, later that day, I tactfully asked a few questions about her background. I learned that after graduating from a University in Kampala, she had gotten her master's degree from the London School of Economics. Then she had worked for a multinational corporation for a few years before deciding that she really wanted to help the poor in her own country. She had given up her prosperous life in Kampala to live among the poor in a modest wooden shack in this rural community. If anything, she was way overqualified for her job, and I had totally misjudged her.

With my Wharton MBA and American lens, I had a specific idea of what a talented financial executive looked like. Because of my preconceptions, I foolishly jumped to some conclusions about her capabilities. But that's how biases distort and hobble our leadership in unhealthy ways. When we prejudge people based on things like gender, race, nationality—even height, weight, or appearance—we fail to leverage the wonderful diversity of gifts and talents God has placed around us.

If you don't think you have these biases, you are probably wrong, because we all have them. And if you are seeking to be a self-aware leader, you will take time to better understand both the specific challenges women, minorities, and people from different age groups face in your workplace environment, and the powerful way diverse experiences and perspectives can shape your organization.

THE PLANK IN YOUR EYE

Jesus' familiar admonition to take the plank out of our own eye before we seek to remove the speck in someone else's is very much about self-awareness. Let's look at this important passage.

> Do not judge, or you too will be judged. For in the same way you judge others, you will be judged, and with the measure you use, it will be measured to you.
>
> Why do you look at the speck of sawdust in your brother's eye and pay no attention to the plank in your own eye? How can you say to your brother, "Let me take the speck out of your eye," when all the time there is a plank in your own eye? You hypocrite, first take the plank

out of your own eye, and then you will see clearly to remove the speck from your brother's eye. (Matthew 7:1-5)

Jesus tells us that if we want to *see clearly*, it starts with self-awareness; we first must acknowledge and remove the "plank" from our own eye. In other words, before we judge others (or lead others), we need to take a long, hard look at our own shortcomings and motives. This process is meant to be humbling, as we realize how many flaws, deficiencies, and biases we ourselves possess. And only when we have done a fair assessment of our own deficiencies are we in the proper state of mind to see clearly those of our coworkers. But now we will see them with much more empathy and compassion.

As you seek to become a better leader, be aware of the effect you have on the others around you. Put yourself in their shoes and try to assess the impact of your words and your tone of voice before you speak. Get to know more about your team members—their backgrounds, families, passions, and interests. Make a point to know whether they are going through tough times outside the workplace. Are their kids doing well, are they caring for aging parents, is their spouse struggling with a medical challenge? When you get to know them in this way you will be much more effective in being their leader and bringing out the best in them.

The people you work with were placed in your life for a reason. You have been entrusted with them for a season. God wants you to be his ambassador in their lives, showing them his love and care. A leader who embodies the values outlined in this book—integrity, humility, generosity, love, forgiveness, self-awareness, and so on— creates an environment that makes team members feel safe and secure rather than fearful and paranoid. And people who feel safe and secure tend to perform at their highest level.

BALANCE

ALL WORK AND NO PLAY

SCRIPTURE ➤ "Very early in the morning, while it was still dark, Jesus got up, left the house and went off to a solitary place, where he prayed. Simon and his companions went to look for him, and when they found him, they exclaimed: 'Everyone is looking for you!'" (Mark 1:35-37)

"But Jesus often withdrew to lonely places and prayed." (Luke 5:15-16)

LEADERSHIP PRINCIPLE ➤ A leader who achieves a healthy balance in life between work, family, faith, and rest will broaden their perspective, make better decisions, and set a positive example for their teams.

> *Work is a rubber ball. If you drop it, it will bounce back. But the other four balls—family, health, friends and spirit—are made of glass. If you drop one of these, they will be irrevocably scuffed, marked, nicked, damaged or even shattered.*
>
> **BRYAN DYSON**

I STILL VIVIDLY REMEMBER one particular Halloween. It was the Halloween when I risked my career for a few bags of candy.

At the time, Reneé and I had five children ages two to fourteen, and they were all quite excited about putting on their costumes to go trick-or-treating that evening. I promised to be home in time to join them. I was the COO at Lenox and had an important gathering that day at work. The CEO (my boss) had called an all-hands-on-deck meeting of the senior leadership to make a critical decision about the future of our crystal factory in Pennsylvania. A decision had to made about whether we would have to close the factory for financial reasons.

I believe the meeting started around nine in the morning, and about twenty-five of us gathered in the board room to hear multiple presentations and analyses before making the decision. The issue was complex, and the meeting kept extending: two hours, four hours, six hours and still going. It was intense. At about five o'clock I looked at my watch and realized that my commitment to be with Reneé and my kids for Halloween was in jeopardy. But I was still hopeful. Surely the meeting would end soon. But by six o'clock the CEO showed no signs of adjourning to the following day. That's when I decided to do the unthinkable. I raised my hand, and the CEO recognized me. "Jim," I said, "today is Halloween, and I have five little kids at home waiting for their dad to take them trick-or-treating. I'm afraid I need to leave the meeting now. But I will be in tomorrow morning bright and early to continue this discussion with you." I could almost hear an audible gasp as twenty-plus VPs and division presidents watched one of their colleagues do the unimaginable—put his family ahead of his career. I knew that most of them had kids waiting at home for them too, but I had been the one foolhardy enough to actually say it.

There was a pregnant pause as the room quieted and the CEO (and everyone else) looked over at me. And here it came. "Why Rich,

I had totally forgotten that today was Halloween. I don't have little kids at home anymore. You need to go and be with your family. I can bring you up to speed in the morning." Whew! I thanked him for understanding, got up, and left the room. But everyone else stayed for the next two hours.

I made a choice that day. But it was a choice I had made years before—that my marriage, my family, and my faith would always take priority over my work. Now, I certainly didn't live this out perfectly. My three million miles of air travel during my time at World Vision caused me to miss far too many soccer games, clarinet recitals, and just time hanging out with my kids. I even missed some critical doctor appointments for my wife when I should have been there. But my overriding mindset was that I would fight to have the right balance in my life, and that fight was a continual struggle. But I have learned that if you're not willing to fight for a healthy balance in your life, you just won't have it.

WHAT ARE YOUR WALNUTS?

Reneé uses an illustration with some of her women's Bible study groups around how to think about having a healthy and balanced life in the midst of many competing demands. She takes a glass jar, a quantity of rice, and five or six walnuts. The jar represents the finite amount of time we have in our lives. The walnuts represent the big, important things in life that we need to make time for: devotional time with the Lord, our marriages, our children, our friends, service to others, rest, and so on. The rice represents all the other many demands on our time.

First, she pours the rice into the jar. Next, she tries to put in all the walnuts. You guessed it, not all the walnuts will fit. But then she reverses the order, putting the walnuts—life's most important things—in first, followed by the rice. Now it all fits because the rice manages to fill all the spaces among and between the walnuts. The key point is that you have to start with the walnuts. Ideally, this is the way we should order our lives, starting with the things that matter most. But sometimes not all the walnuts will fit, and it creates tension.

In today's work environment, where connectivity is 24-7, establishing boundaries between work and life is exceedingly difficult. Twenty- and thirtysomethings today face a workplace totally different from the one I experienced early in my career. Work follows you home every day, stays with you on the weekends, and even goes on vacation with you. You're often expected to be available at all hours to answer emails, texts, and phone calls. The result can be a blurring of life and work, which can be both stressful and harmful in the long run. There aren't easy choices here. If you work in that kind of environment, you need to try to establish healthy boundaries. Sometimes that just involves you making healthier choices, but if the demands on you are out of your control, it requires you to have a difficult conversation with your boss about your workload and his or her expectations of you. You might be surprised and find that your boss is more understanding than you think. Good bosses can and should help establish healthy boundaries for the people on their team by not imposing or expecting 24-7 availability.

Achieving a healthy work-life balance can be especially difficult for women in light of the disproportionate responsibility traditionally placed on them for childcare and management of the home. According to a recent study, women perform about four hours of unpaid work in the home each day compared to just two and a half hours for men—that's 60 percent more. In effect, women have two demanding jobs, but only one job pays a salary. The result is that they must struggle even harder to maintain any semblance of balance in their lives. The choices this forces women to make can be stressful.

However, a leader who is sensitive to these issues in the workplace can make reasonable accommodations for staff, whether male or female, who are trying to balance the demands of the workplace with the demands of family. Simple things like allowing an employee a late start if children need to be dropped off at school or to work some hours from home can make a huge difference in improving work-life balance. And employees who are afforded these considerations will be less stressed, more productive, and more loyal to an employer who values them enough to care. You can also model a healthy life balance by leaving the workplace at a reasonable time, not answering emails and texts on weekends, and demonstrating the importance of a healthy life outside the workplace. You as a leader have both the opportunity and the responsibility to help your team manage their work-life tensions satisfactorily.

HARD CHOICES

Achieving an acceptable work-life balance will likely require you to make difficult choices and establish some firm boundaries, even if there might be consequences. When I was in my twenties and working at Parker Brothers, Reneé and I had volunteered to lead the grade-school children's recreation program, called Discoverers, at our church. It went from five to seven on Friday nights plus one Saturday a month. So, I would have to leave the office every Friday at 4:30 to get there on time.

That year, when it came time for my annual performance review, my boss told me I was not likely to get promoted based on his view that I was not committed enough to the job. I was shocked because I thought I had been doing really well. But, as I listened, most of his criticisms were not related to the caliber of my work but rather to the image I was projecting to senior management—my beard was unprofessional, I wasn't "dressing the part," and I wasn't schmoozing with the right people in the lunch room. Then he pointed out that leaving early on Fridays for a "church thing" showed that I wasn't putting the job first. We discussed each of these issues, and I told him that I would work on the things he listed. But I took a risk and told him that I wouldn't give up the kids' program at church. Volunteering at church was one of my "walnuts." I remember saying that since we both worked for a toy company, it was kind of ironic that I was being criticized for volunteering to work with a group of children. Weren't they our core customers?

In the months that followed I shaved my beard, bought some new suits, worked a little harder at the corporate politics, and managed to bring myself back into good standing again. But I took the risk of continuing to participate in the kids' program at church every Friday. A couple of years later that boss left the company, and I got promoted to his job. While my story had a happy ending, yours may be different, and only you can decide what lines you can afford to draw based on your workplace reality and demands of your life outside work. But if you don't draw those lines, you will never achieve the right balance in your life.

There is a postscript to my story about the children's ministry. Almost forty years later I was invited to preach at the church where our son Pete was serving as the junior high youth pastor. As people came up to greet me and Reneé after the service one man, who looked to be in his early fifties, came up and asked whether I remembered him.

Turns out he was one of the boys in that kids' program we had led all those years ago in Boston. He had grown up, gotten married, and now lived in the Chicago area. Then he told me that his son was now part of our son Pete's junior high youth group, and that Pete was making a real difference in his son's life. Wow! Our efforts from almost forty years earlier had now come full circle. The seeds we had sown had sprouted. I had drawn a line to protect my commitment at church, and God had paid it forward in a way I could never have imagined.

THE OPPOSITE OF BALANCE— THE WORKAHOLIC

There is another cause of poor work-life balance that is not externally imposed but self-imposed. Workaholism is an all-too-common malady. In the high-pressure culture found in many work environments today, the workaholic becomes a kind of tragic hero. He or she is the person who will sacrifice anything for the cause. But the cause is usually pretty mundane in the scheme of things: selling more stuff, building a stronger brand, or—one of my favorites— increasing shareholder value.

When I worked at Lenox, selling fine china and crystal to those who could afford it, I had a small sign on my desk that said: "Relax, It's Only Dishes." It was an attempt to put our periodic "crises" in perspective. After all, there are few true emergencies in our world that involve fine china. As I previously mentioned, the other slogan I lived by was "This too shall pass." It was important to realize that today's "crisis" would likely not be remembered at all ten years from now. But missing your daughter's soccer championship or your spouse's birthday, not once but again and again, will matter in ten years—and not in a good way.

171

The late US Senator Paul Tsongas, among others, was credited with saying: "Nobody on his deathbed ever said: I wish I had spent more time at the office." There's something about envisioning one's deathbed that has a way of bringing clarity to the day-to-day decisions we are making right now. Essentially, workaholics make a deal with the devil: they exchange short-term gains in their work for long-term tragedies in their lives, as they become consumed by the "tyranny of the urgent."

WORKAHOLICS MAKE A DEAL WITH THE DEVIL: THEY EXCHANGE SHORT-TERM GAINS IN THEIR WORK FOR LONG-TERM TRAGEDIES IN THEIR LIVES.

The founder of World Vision, Bob Pierce, was a workaholic. He became so driven and so obsessed with "doing the Lord's work" by helping the poor that he neglected other important things in his life. In conversations I had with his widow, Lorraine, and his daughter, Marilee, I learned about the heavy price his family paid for his obsessive behavior. They told me that for more than twenty consecutive years, he traveled internationally about nine months out of the year, many of those trips lasting for months at a time. Like many of his generation, Pierce was motivated by an all-consuming drive to reach the lost for Christ and a huge vision to help the poor in Jesus' name. Unfortunately, that vision often left him blind to the needs of those closest to him. And while his efforts did result in the creation of World Vision, an organization that has helped millions of people, it came with consequences. He became estranged from his wife and family, losing his marriage. And in 1967, seventeen years after founding World Vision, he was asked to resign by the World Vision board because of his increasingly erratic leadership style. Tragically, Bob Pierce's life lacked any semblance of balance.

In my first year leading World Vision I was drawn into this same kind of obsessive behavior—spending long hours at the office and traveling constantly. I justified it just as Bob Pierce had, by reasoning that children's lives and souls were at stake. It wasn't just dishes. At the same time, Reneé was trying to help our five children adjust to leaving all their friends behind and moving to a new community and a new school. My wife and kids really needed a husband and father right then, but I was too absorbed to see it. Finally, Reneé had a talk with me. She said, "I am only going to say this once. Our kids need a full-time dad right now. They will never be able to compete with needy children all around the world, and it's not fair to expect them to. You need to figure out how to do your job and still be a father to your own children." She was right, of course, and as I reflected on this, I realized that my own workaholism stemmed from an underlying belief that somehow God could not use World Vision for his purposes unless I was there to make it happen. I had to be in every meeting, fly to meet every donor, see the work in every country, and "parachute in" to every natural disaster. And if I didn't do those things, then God's work might just fail.

Not only was that arrogant, it was a kind of idolatry, the belief that I was somehow more important to the work than God himself. This affliction is especially common to those who are involved in full-time ministry, and I want to offer a word of caution to you if you're serving in that capacity. Don't justify your obsessive behavior because you are "doing God's work." Believe it or not, God, and your ministry, can succeed without you. And God does not call us to abandon our other important responsibilities, using him as our excuse.

In my opinion, workaholism at its core is a form of self-importance that believes nobody else can do it if I'm not involved, that nothing will succeed if my hands haven't touched it. That attitude also sends a terrible message to the team that you are leading—that they just aren't good enough to do it without you. And your poor example will put pressure on them to adopt your damaging work habits. The best leaders leverage the gifts and abilities of the entire team so that no single individual has to carry an inordinate share of the work.

THE BALANCED LEADER

The opposite of the workaholic is the balanced leader. But why is balance so important for a leader to have in their life? First, it's important to understand that balance means a lot more than just spending time with your family, though that is critically important. A balanced life is well-rounded in multiple dimensions. For a leader to be at their best, they need to have clear minds, stability outside the workplace, positive relationships with both family and friends, and a sense of meaning and purpose not solely derived from work.

A BALANCED LIFE IS WELL-ROUNDED IN MULTIPLE DIMENSIONS.

For the Christian leader, purpose and identity are found first in our relationship with God and our one job to know, love, and serve him in this life. As Christ's ambassadors, we are on mission in our workplaces. That means we need to make adequate time for worship, prayer, Scripture, devotions, and service. These things remind us of who we belong to and connect us to the deeper purpose and meaning of our work.

In Mark 1 we see one of the many times that Jesus withdrew from his work to spend time in prayer, reconnecting with his Father in heaven: "Very early in the morning, while it was still dark, Jesus got up, left the house and went off to a solitary place, where he prayed. Simon and his companions went to look for him, and when they found him, they exclaimed: 'Everyone is looking for you!'" (Mark 1:35-37). We must remember the tremendous pressure Jesus was under in his work. He had become a visible public figure with throngs of people following him everywhere. In this chapter alone he called his first disciples, cast out demons, healed multitudes, and preached in front of large crowds of people. In the very next chapter, he was accused of blasphemy by the religious leaders. And we think our jobs are stressful? Yet we are told here, and in many other places in the Gospels, that Jesus withdrew from the limelight, went off by himself, and spent time in prayer and meditation with the Father. Simon Peter and the other disciples were irritated at him when they found him, exclaiming: "Everyone is looking for you!" But Jesus understood that his mission was so critical he had to make time to get away from the demands placed on him so that he could align himself with the Father's purposes. Jesus was seeking balance in his life. And in the same way, we as Christ's ambassadors must also withdraw from the many stresses in our lives to align with the Father's purposes. If we are spiritually out of balance, everything else in our life will be negatively affected. Our time with God is perhaps the most important "walnut" in our jar.

> **IF WE ARE SPIRITUALLY OUT OF BALANCE, EVERYTHING ELSE IN OUR LIFE WILL BE NEGATIVELY AFFECTED.**

BALANCE IS ALSO ABOUT PERSPECTIVE

But achieving balance in our lives only starts with our "God time." It also requires that we make time for family, friendships, service, reading, rest, and recreation. And this kind of diversification of our lives has another important benefit for leaders: it gives us a broader perspective. If our life is our work and our work is our life, we live in a very small world. It's easy to lose perspective on the bigger picture and our higher purpose when we sink into work-related tunnel vision.

You may be surprised to see reading on my list of things necessary for a balanced life. I want to unpack that a bit because I have come to believe that being an avid reader is something that makes all leaders better. President Harry Truman once said: "Not all readers are leaders, but all leaders are readers." Warren Buffett spends five to six hours a day reading five newspapers and five hundred pages of corporate reports. Bill Gates reads fifty books a year. Mark Zuckerberg reads at least one book every two weeks. Elon Musk grew up reading two books a day.

Investing precious time in reading opens up a whole world of wisdom and experiences beyond your own. And I'm not talking about just reading books on leadership! During my career I tried to read a broad spectrum of things including novels, biographies, historical nonfiction, thrillers, classics, and a couple of newspapers. One year I read *Moby Dick, Frankenstein*, biographies of Winston Churchill and Steve Jobs, several good contemporary novels, a couple of books by theologian N. T. Wright, and a book by journalist Malcolm Gladwell.

Now some of you are protesting, saying that you just don't have time to read. I felt that way too until I realized that I could listen to audiobooks or podcasts on my commute, on airplanes, when I was exercising, or when I was working around the house. It is a great way to redeem the time you spend doing otherwise perfunctory tasks. And today, almost everything, including major newspapers, is available in audio format.

Reading can make you a better leader because it exercises different "muscles" in your brain. It provides you with a much broader perspective and reference frame within which to better process work-related situations. Reading is also about lifelong learning, and it will make you a better student, a better teacher, and a more interesting person to talk with. Last, reading is a form of escape and retreat from the pressures of the workplace. I can't tell you how many times I sat in the garage for an extra couple of minutes when I got home from work because the book I was listening to in my car was so engaging. It helped me unplug and put the hassles of the day behind me so I could be more present with my family when I came home.

A more balanced perspective affects the way we see the world and how our work fits into the other dimensions of our lives. Leaders who are more grounded, who have a broader outlook on their life and work, ultimately are more positive, are more productive, and make better decisions. A well-ordered life is like ballast in the hold of a ship. It provides stability and security, especially when the waters get choppy.

For a leader to be at their best, they need to have clear minds, stability outside the workplace, positive relationships with both family and friends, and a sense of meaning and purpose not solely derived from work. God calls us as leaders to model the abundant life. As Jesus said, "I have come that they may have life, and that they may have it more abundantly" (John 10:10 NKJV).

HUMOR

IF WE DON'T LAUGH, WE'LL CRY

SCRIPTURE ➤

"There is a time for everything,
and a season for every activity under the heavens . . .
a time to weep and a time to laugh,
a time to mourn and a time to dance." (Ecclesiastes 3:1,4)

LEADERSHIP PRINCIPLE ➤ A leader who uses humor well has a powerful, culture-shaping tool that can ease tension, relieve stress, and bring a healthy perspective to workplace challenges. Humor is a gift you can give to those you lead.

A sense of humor is part of the art of leadership,
of getting along with people, of getting things done.

DWIGHT D. EISENHOWER

A sense of humor is God's antidote for anger and frustration.

RICK WARREN

Iᴛ ᴡᴀs ᴀ ᴄʀɪᴛɪᴄᴀʟ ɴɪɴᴇ ᴏ'ᴄʟᴏᴄᴋ ᴍᴇᴇᴛɪɴɢ. The top brass from Toys "R" Us had gathered in the Parker Brothers showroom at the New York Toy Fair to make their buying commitments for the fall season. They were our biggest customer, and this was our one chance to sell them our new product line. But our key player, Dick, my boss and the vice president of marketing, who was supposed to lead the meeting, didn't show up. I and a couple of other lower-level managers waited nervously for the boss to arrive as the Toys "R" Us executives looked at their watches with impatience. Then someone opened the conference room door and passed me a note. It was a message from Dick. He was unavoidably detained and would be at least a half an hour late. I was to start the meeting without him. And so, I made apologies to our guests and proceeded to present our new fall product line to our single biggest customer.

By the time Dick finally showed up, the meeting had ended and the Toys "R" Us buyers had left. Not showing up for the meeting with our largest customer had been a major faux pas, and the other VPs were not happy. Dick came in sweating and flustered and proceeded to tell us his tale of woe. The hotel where we were staying had an overnight shoe-shining service. If you put your shoes outside your door at night, the hotel staff would polish them and return them before morning. But Dick's shoes hadn't been returned, and they were the only pair he had brought. It was winter, and he couldn't very well come to the meeting in stocking feet. And the shoe stores didn't open until nine. So, he gave some money to one of the hotel staff and sent them out to buy him a pair of size eleven black dress shoes the moment the shoe store opened. When the shoes finally arrived, he rushed across town, hoping to join the meeting in progress. But it was too late.

Dick was obviously distraught, and the room was tense, but somehow I managed to find some humor in the situation. Impulsively, I reached under the table, slipped off my very similar size-eleven black dress shoes, lifted them up and pushed them toward Dick. Pretending remorse, I said: "Dick, I am so sorry. I shouldn't have taken them. It was a terrible practical joke. I didn't realize how much trouble it would cause." There was an audible gasp around the table. Dick, eyes wide, looked at me with a mixture of disbelief and rage. And then . . . he realized I was just messing with him. The entire room, including Dick, erupted with laughter, and the mood shifted from somber to raucous as we all had a good laugh together. Then we debriefed what had happened at the meeting and went on with our day—crisis passed.

Humor is a powerful tool in a leader's tool kit. It builds camaraderie and team spirit. In the midst of difficulty, it can bring relief and a healthier outlook. It helps us face our most difficult challenges without despairing. The poet Lord Byron said: "Always laugh when you can. It is cheap medicine." And medicine it is. Medical studies have shown that laughter produces chemical effects in our bodies that reduce pain, lower stress, and even strengthen our immune system. Humor helps us put difficult problems and situations in perspective. It provides us a coping mechanism when we are overwhelmed by something happening in our lives. And as a leader humor is a gift you can give to those you lead.

A leader who uses humor puts people at ease. Humor can break the ice in a meeting where people are not well acquainted because it taps into our universal human experience. A team that laughs together is in a much better frame of mind to work together with trust and shared purpose.

Humor even bridges cultural gaps. I remember meeting an African great-grandmother named Finedia in Zambia. Finedia was raising her only great-granddaughter by herself because all her children *and* grandchildren had died of AIDS. Her situation was tragic. And here I came into her meager mud-and-thatch hut, a large white man from America who couldn't be more different from her. But Finedia and I had one thing in common—we both had a full head of white hair. I reached up and touched my own hair; then I reached out and touched hers and said through our translator: "We are the same. We both have white hair and the Bible tells us that white hair is a crown of glory!" Finedia gave me a wide smile, and we both had a hearty laugh. After that, we were just friends and we talked at length about her family, her sadness, and her precious great-granddaughter, Maggie. Victor Borge was right when he said, "Laughter is the shortest distance between two people."

A TEAM THAT LAUGHS TOGETHER IS IN A MUCH BETTER FRAME OF MIND TO WORK TOGETHER.

I THINK JESUS LIKED TO LAUGH

When we read the Gospels, we don't see a lot of references to Jesus laughing or making others laugh. But I suspect that this is because writing with humor in the first century, especially about such a serious topic, would have been culturally inappropriate. But the Gospels do paint a picture of Jesus as a warm and welcoming person. His very first miracle was to turn water into wine at a wedding. That whole episode showed his penchant for the ironic—the Son of God using his powers to keep a party going! And he regularly participated in banquets and parties, often provoking criticism from the religious leaders. He sang songs and told story after story to the people who gathered around him as he taught them about God. He used hyperbole in telling people not to take the speck out of their neighbor's eye until they removed the plank from their own. And picturing that camel trying to get through the eye of the needle had to provoke a few guffaws. Jesus also welcomed children into his midst. In the feeding of the five thousand, he played a mind game on his grousing disciples, who complained about the impracticality of feeding so many people. So Jesus took a young boy's lunch and multiplied it to feed the crowd. The punch line came when he asked the disciples to collect the leftovers: twelve basketfuls, one souvenir for each of the doubting disciples. I think Jesus might just have chuckled about that. I have no doubt that while Jesus had a serious mission, he also had a warm, welcoming, and cheerful disposition when he mingled with people daily.

LAUGHING AT WORK

But we have to be careful with humor too. Humor in the workplace has to be gentle and not biting. And as a Christian you must resist the temptation to fall into the coarse and vulgar humor and language that characterizes most secular work environments. Indulging in that kind of coarseness will undermine all your efforts to demonstrate the character of Christ to your coworkers.

HUMOR IN THE WORKPLACE HAS TO BE GENTLE AND NOT BITING.

Humor can be uplifting, but it can also be weaponized to hurt people. Early in our marriage I remember joking around with our couples' Bible study group, getting laughs sometimes at my wife's expense. One night when we came home, she was terribly upset with me. "You think you're funny, but when your jokes are about me, it's hurtful. I don't want to be the butt of your jokes." That was a powerful lesson. If you

HUMOR CAN BE UPLIFTING, BUT IT CAN ALSO BE WEAPONIZED TO HURT PEOPLE.

use humor to embarrass or humiliate a coworker, it can be devastating, especially if you are the boss. Make the humor about the situation or circumstances your team finds them-

selves in. Your humor should be good-hearted. Even better is when a leader pokes fun at themselves and shows that they don't take themselves too seriously.

THE "SHROUD OF TURIN"

I remember making a ridiculous blunder on a trip to Nashville where I was to meet with the governor of Tennessee and then speak to eighteen hundred church leaders. I had flown in from Seattle and gotten an Uber from the airport to take me to the convention center. I was running late and barely going to make my meeting with the governor. But instead of telling the driver to take me to the convention center on Fifth Avenue, I told him Fifth Street, which turns out to be a completely different part of town. So, by the time we course-corrected and I finally reached the convention center, I was running into the building—and I mean I literally *ran into* the building. The huge glass wall at the entry had looked to me like an open doorway, so I ran headlong into the glass! It was kind of like when a bird flies into your window—*thunk!* At ramming speed, I hit the glass face first and bounced three feet backward, dropping everything I was carrying. I was stunned. People who saw it happen rushed over to see if I was all right. I made like it was no big deal and waved them off. My nose and face were numb, and my head was throbbing, but the governor was waiting, so I hopped on the escalator and headed toward the meeting area. But the convention center was huge, and I had no idea just where the meeting room was located. So, at the top of the escalator I asked someone for directions. He looked at me with alarm and said, "Mister, are you ok? Your nose is bleeding." Oh, great! I managed to find a restroom and looked in the mirror. The bridge of my nose had split wide open, and blood was pouring out of it. My whole face was red and blotchy from the impact—I was definitely not ready for public viewing.

A dozen paper towels later I had cleaned up as best I could and hopped on the next escalator, holding a wet compress on my nose. At the top of the steps a team of World Vision people were waiting for me. Here came the boss with a blotchy face, a bright red and bleeding nose, and a rather disoriented look. "What happened to you?" they asked. I think I said, "You should see the other guy." Then I explained what had happened. When I told them that I was certain that I had left a "Shroud of Turin" imprint of my face on that glass panel, we all started to laugh at my misfortune. They sent someone out to buy bandages and then took me to the governor. And yeah, I had to tell him the whole story too. When we all left the convention center that evening, we walked by the scene of the crime and sure enough, there on the glass was a clear oily impression of my eyes, my nose, and my mouth, twisted into a grimace of surprise and pain. The Shroud of Turin indeed. Everybody started laughing again, and one of them even took a picture of the imprint so they could share it on social media. The next week, still bandaged, I shared the story in our weekly chapel, and everybody had a good laugh on me.

Self-deprecating humor makes a leader more human, more approachable, and more relatable to the people on their team. For most of my years at World Vision I dressed up in a Santa costume, complete with beard, before Christmas. I went throughout our buildings distributing Christmas cookies and some good cheer. For maximum effect, I wore special "ruby slippers"—shoes that my assistant had coated with red glitter—and red, star-shaped glasses á la Elton John. I was accompanied on my rounds by a few members of my senior staff whom I forced to dress as elves. Lots of staff wanted selfies with Santa and his elves, and it gave people a good laugh during our busiest and most stressful fundraising season.

We laughed a lot during my years leading World Vision. But, ironically, one of my original apprehensions about taking the job twenty years earlier was that I would have to leave my sense of humor at the door.

SELF-DEPRECATING HUMOR MAKES A LEADER MORE HUMAN.

Humor was so much a part of my leadership style that I felt like I would die in an environment that was always deadly serious. In an organization that every day must face poverty, suffering, and tragedy, I imagined a humorless culture in which laughter was inappropriate. But I was wrong. It was just the opposite. In a ministry confronted by human suffering every day, laughter is desperately needed. It is therapy. It is restorative. People were hungry for an occasional laugh that could bring them needed relief.

Every week when I opened up our chapel service with various announcements, I always tried to lift everyone's spirits with a little humor. My five minutes of "stand-up" became something people looked forward to. It brought us together—hundreds of us all gathered in a big room. We had a serious mission, and everyone needed a break from the heaviness. It has been said that sometimes if we don't laugh, we'll cry. And in the midst of stress or grief or difficult circumstances, a little levity can minister to the people you work with. Martin Luther, the serious guy who started the Reformation and broke with the Catholic Church, was not known for his humor. But listen to what he once said: "If I am not allowed to laugh in heaven, I don't want to go there." I couldn't agree more.

17

ENCOURAGEMENT

WELL DONE, GOOD AND FAITHFUL SERVANT

SCRIPTURE ➤ "Therefore encourage one another and build each other up, just as in fact you are doing. Now we ask you, brothers and sisters, to acknowledge those who work hard among you, who care for you in the Lord and who admonish you. Hold them in the highest regard in love because of their work." (1 Thessalonians 5:11-13)

LEADERSHIP PRINCIPLE ➤ A leader who understands the power of encouragement and affirmation will see a huge return on investment, paid back in improved performance, motivation, and loyalty.

In our postmodern world people have been treated as numbers, as replaceable parts, as something on someone's agenda, a program, a screen name. They long to be noticed, to be valued, to have someone pay attention!

LEIGHTON FORD

Treat a man as he is and he will remain as he is. Treat a man as he can and should be and he will become as he can and should be.

STEPHEN R. COVEY

I STARTED PLAYING GOLF when I was in my teens with a cheap set of clubs that I bought at the grocery store. Though I was never very good at golf, I couldn't really blame the clubs; it was the archer who was at fault, not the bow and arrow. But golf was something fun to do outside with my friends, so we would play at a public course whenever we could during the summer. My golf swing featured a long list of mechanical flaws, but my signature symptom was a wicked and consistent slice. Every one of my drives curved sharply to the right, usually into the woods, an adjacent fairway, or a body of water. I learned to automatically yell "Fore!" as soon as I hit the ball. This was the only part of my golf game that I could always rely on. Of course, it never dawned on me to take a lesson from a more accomplished golfer to see whether my slice could be corrected.

But sometime in my early forties—thirty years too late—I did take a lesson. The instructor asked me to hit a few balls and immediately noticed my slice. "How long have you had that slice?" he asked. "Pretty much since the first time I picked up a club," I said. The instructor handed me a tee and said, "Put this tee under your left armpit and hold it there. Then, when you swing, try to make sure the tee doesn't fall out." I hit my next five drives straight down the fairway. This simple trick had corrected my problem by forcing me to rotate my body fully through the swing, thereby hitting the ball squarely and without the dreaded spin that sent my drives careening to the right. If only I had learned this simple trick thirty years earlier. Who knows, maybe I would have become a professional golfer!

The unfortunate thing about wisdom is that by the time you've finally acquired it, it's often too late to make a difference. A former CEO and friend who is now in his eighties opined to me that he now knows most of the answers, but sadly no one is asking him the questions anymore.

When I speak about leadership issues today, I am sometimes asked what one thing I would have done differently in my career if I had known at the beginning what I know now. There are a few things I could say in response, but my number-one answer is this: I wish I had better understood the power of encouragement to motivate others, lift performance, and help the people around me realize their full, God-given potential. That simple tip could have improved my "leadership slice" and kept me out of some woods and water hazards. The best leaders know that regular affirmation and encouragement, not criticism, is what helps the people on their team develop confidence, improve their performance, and lean into their gifts and abilities. Encouragement energizes people, while criticism often demoralizes.

This shouldn't come as a surprise. If you have children, you probably do this naturally. When Jonny makes the JV soccer team at school, we praise his athletic abilities. When young Susie gets an A in math, we talk about what a great scientist or engineer she may someday be. We say these things to our children because we want them to see what's possible. We want them to understand and develop their gifts and talents and to gain confidence in themselves.

> **ENCOURAGEMENT ENERGIZES PEOPLE, WHILE CRITICISM OFTEN DEMORALIZES.**

When most of us think back on why our lives turned out the way they did, we can often look back on moments when a little positive encouragement made a huge difference in our self-confidence. But the corollary is also true. There were also moments of sharp criticism from a teacher, parent, or boss that devastated our self-esteem and caused great harm.

miss taylor
: telling thrason is was stupid
and dumb.

191

THE CRITIC AND THE ENCOURAGER

In chapter five I wrote about leaving my very first job out of business school, at Gillette, to go to Parker Brothers. It was the episode that taught me a lot about trusting God. But let me now elaborate a bit more on that story because it also taught me a profound lesson about encouragement.

Given my family background, entering the Fortune 500 corporate culture at Gillette was as foreign to me as if I had moved to Ethiopia. Most of my peers had Harvard, Wharton, or Stanford MBAs and came out of professional families. They had grown up in affluence and been bred to become captains of industry. My father, on the other hand, had an eighth-grade education and sold used cars. My mother was a filing clerk who never finished high school. And so I was both unprepared for corporate life and a little rough around the edges.

When I was hired at Gillette, I was told that after my first year I could transfer from the sales department into the marketing department to join one of the brand-marketing teams. Marketing was my first love so, after about eighteen months on the job, I went to human resources and asked how I might make the transfer happen. The HR vice president, Walter, said he would set up a couple of interviews for me with the marketing directors. A few days after those interviews he called me in. "Rich, I'm afraid marketing is not in the cards for you. The marketing directors just don't think you have the right stuff to succeed in brand management. But you can still have a fine career in sales." I was devastated. Apparently, my rough edges had been noticed. I was twenty-five years old, and my dream was already being crushed. In the next weeks I updated my résumé and started looking for a marketing job at a different company. As I shared in chapter five, I sent just one résumé out, responding to a want ad placed by Parker Brothers Games for an entry-level marketing job. I applied, was called for interviews, and a couple weeks later I got the job! I was on cloud nine.

The next week I went back to Walter's office to tell him I was resigning, explaining that at Parker Brothers I could work in marketing. His parting words were the opposite of encouragement. "Rich, you're making a big mistake. You don't have what it takes to succeed in marketing, and besides, it's a young person's game, and you're already two years behind your peers. You're going to regret this." I don't have what it takes? A young person's game? Is twenty-five really too old for a job change? Again, I felt demoralized and wondered secretly if maybe he was right; maybe I didn't have what it took. Self-doubt crept in.

Nevertheless, two weeks later I reported for duty at Parker Brothers ready to give it my best. Fortunately Ed, my new boss, turned out to be an encourager. He gave me lots of different assignments that frankly I wasn't ready for, assuring me that I could figure them out. When I brought him some of my early progress, he praised me enthusiastically, asked me a few additional questions, and then sent me back out to get those answers. When I would finish one assignment, he'd give me something harder to do. He helped me believe that there was nothing I couldn't accomplish.

When we needed to shoot a TV commercial in New York for one of our new games, he took me with him to learn. It opened up a whole new world for me as I saw how the whole process worked. A few weeks later we needed to shoot another spot for our new word game, Boggle, and he told me I could take the lead and go do it without him. "Are you serious?" I asked. A commercial shoot involved hundreds of thousands of dollars and dozens of people from the ad agency and the production company. I was twenty-five years old! "Sure, you can do it," he said. "I've watched you, and you've got what it takes. No problem. Call me if you need me for anything." And so I flew to New York and managed the entire shoot for the TV commercial for Boggle, which is still a bestseller today.

Can you see the difference between Walter and Ed? Walter was a critic, while Ed was an encourager. Walter focused on why I couldn't succeed, while Ed helped me believe I could. And it made all the difference.

Stephen Covey once said: "Treat a man as he is and he will remain as he is. Treat a man as he can and should be and he will become as he can and should be." Ed helped me to become all that I could be. He helped me to realize my God-given potential. Sadly, I only got to work for Ed two years before he left for a different job, but five years after Ed left, I was named president of Parker Brothers. In my mind, I still give Ed the credit because he was the one who showed me what was possible.

There is a delicious postscript to this story. About fifteen years later, when I was president of Lenox, I received a phone call from an executive recruiter. He said his name was Walter. You got it—the same Walter from my days at Gillette, who was now a headhunter. After his introduction, he said that he thought I would be a great fit for a CEO job he was trying to fill. He flattered me with some comments about my great résumé and track record and then he mentioned that we had apparently both worked at Gillette at about the same time, but he didn't remember me. "Let me refresh your memory," I said. And I recounted the story of how he told me I wasn't cut out for marketing, that I didn't have what it would take to succeed, and that I was making a big mistake. He seemed flustered and then sheepishly admitted that perhaps he had been wrong in his early assessment of me. Then he still had the nerve to try to persuade me to throw my hat into the ring for the job he was trying to fill. "No, Walter," I said, "I don't think so. I'm probably not cut out for that job either." It's not often in life that you get the chance to have the last laugh. I must admit, it was quite satisfying.

Do we see their Potential in Jesus Eyes

THE CARROT AND THE STICK

The starting point for understanding the power of encouragement in our workplace is how we view the people with whom we work. If we see them just as "human resources," "headcount," or "full-time equivalents"—terrible terms for people made in the image of God— we woefully misunderstand their significance and potential. But if we see them as uniquely and wonderfully made, with attributes and qualities given to them by their Creator, we can begin to unleash the remarkable abilities God has vested in them.

A leader's number-one job is to help release the unique abilities of each member of his or her team so that they can realize their full potential. A coach's role is similar—to help each player optimize their God-given abilities and to then blend all their individual talents to form an effective team. When you embrace this view of your coworkers, encouragement flows more naturally from your lips.

On the other hand, if you look at your coworkers through the lens of their deficits, your tendency will always be to criticize them in order to improve their performance. As a leader, try to see the positives in the people around you and give people the benefit of the doubt. Encouragement is all about using the carrot more often than the stick.

→ Tom Landry Quote: the job of a coach is to make men do what they do not want to do, in order that they can be what they've always wanted to be.

In the book of Proverbs, we find these ancient bits of wisdom:

The words of the reckless pierce like swords,
> but the tongue of the wise brings healing. (Proverbs 12:18)

You can persuade others
> if you are wise
> and speak sensibly.
Kind words are like honey—
> they cheer you up
> and make you feel strong. (Proverbs 16:23-24 CEV)

Reckless words versus kind words, critical words versus encouraging words. In my various leadership roles over the years, I too often fell into the mindset of criticism when managing my people. The annual performance review was the time to point out weaknesses—things that could have been done better. But as I grew older and wiser, I began to understand that it was better to start by praising all the things that a person had done well. Criticism has its place but is much better received when it is cloaked in praise. Most of us are more likely to receive criticism when it is framed within the context of our positive qualities.

MOST OF US ARE MORE LIKELY TO RECEIVE CRITICISM WHEN IT IS FRAMED WITHIN THE CONTEXT OF OUR POSITIVE QUALITIES.

Sandwich approach

Consider these two different track coaches speaking to a member of the high school four-by-four-hundred relay team just after a race:

Coach 1: "We lost the race because you screwed up the handoff. If you don't fix it, we'll never get to the state championship."

Coach 2: "That was one of the best relay legs you have ever run. If you can make your handoff just a little bit smoother, I believe we can win the state championship."

Which coach do you want to run for? When you as the leader emphasize and praise positive attributes and behaviors, your co-worker walks away energized and encouraged, with greater confidence in their ability to contribute to the team. To quote Mary Poppins: "Just a spoonful of sugar helps the medicine go down, in a most delightful way."

THE STICK

So, what do you do when someone on your team consistently fails to carry out their responsibilities despite your affirmation and en-couragement? It is naive to think that every member of the team will always succeed, and sometimes a leader must make the tough de-cision to remove someone from their job. This is never an easy step to take because a person's livelihood is at stake. Terminating someone is one of the hardest things a leader ever does. And I have found that for leaders working in Christian ministry this is even harder. Firing a person whom you pray with and serve with daily is a terrible task. And churches and Christian organizations are more often prone to avoiding these tough personnel decisions, even when they may be necessary for the health of the ministry.

We naturally want to avoid hurting people. But, in truth, removing someone from a role in which they are unable to succeed might be the best thing for them in the long run. When I see someone who is failing in their job despite their best efforts, I like to say, "There are no bad people, only good people in the wrong job." And while that's not totally true (there are some bad people with bad attitudes), it is often true. That person who is failing in their current job might succeed in a different role that is better aligned with their unique background and abilities. Leaving them in a job where they cannot be successful hurts them. In my experience, someone who is drowning in their job knows they are drowning, and helping them to confront that can be like throwing them a life preserver.

Back in my time at Lenox I had a marketing VP named Jason, who was struggling. He had been in the role for a number of years as our market share had steadily declined. And despite various efforts to improve his performance, it became clear that he was not going to succeed in that role. The tough thing was that he was a person everyone liked. He had a great personality and demeanor and a wonderful family. But he was failing in his job. Part of the problem was skill based, but he had also gotten stale in his marketing role after years of doing the same thing. He was in a rut and had run out of fresh ideas and insights.

I had the unpleasant task of sitting down with Jason to give him the terrible news that it was time for him to leave Lenox. He took it hard. He was shocked, hurt, and angry, which is just how most people feel when they lose their job. Having been fired twice myself, I had developed a lot more empathy for people facing the shock of losing their job. I said something like this to him: "Jason, I know you won't want to hear this now, but this could be a beneficial thing for you in the long run. You are a talented guy with a lot to offer. But your approach and your skill set are not what Lenox needs right now for this next season. Sometimes a plant needs to be repotted, not because the plant is bad but because it's gotten rootbound. All it needs to flourish is a new pot and some new soil. I believe that with a fresh start in a different company and culture, you could thrive. A year from now if we meet, I would not be surprised to hear that you have found a new job in a place where you are having great success. Hopefully you will be able to look back and see that this terrible day actually turned out to be a good thing for you." But on that painful day, Jason was having none of it. He was still hurt and angry when he left.

About a year later I went to the annual tabletop show in New York, where all the companies showed their new product lines. While walking through a competitor's showroom I saw Jason across the room. Our eyes met, and we walked toward each other. After an awkward handshake I asked him how he was doing. "Rich," he said, "I am loving my new job and my new company. I've found a real home here, and my Lenox experience is adding a lot of value. I've got a new lease on life. Last year when you told me that being fired might turn out to be a good thing for me, I was angry, and I thought you were crazy. But now, looking back, this change really has been a good thing. And, by the way, I hope you know that we're going to kick your butt in the market this year." Touché!

Now, I can't say that everyone who loses their job will experience what Jason did, but I do believe that caring for your coworkers sometimes involves tough love. In the end, you want them to experience the joy of doing a job in which they can thrive, in a role where their gifts and talents are a better fit.

Once, just after I had been fired from Parker Brothers, I shared my "tragedy" with an older Christian man at church named Tom. His response gobsmacked me: "That's exciting, Rich!"

"Exciting?" I asked, "Really? And why is this exciting?"

"Because at times like these you know God is about to make a big change in your life. And I can't wait to see what he does." I hadn't thought of it quite in those terms, but what a great way to look at setbacks and disappointments in our lives.

THE CARROT

When we look at Simon Peter in the New Testament, we are struck by his many character flaws: impulsive, inconsistent, prone to anger and to speaking before thinking—good old Peter. And, as we know, toward the end, he is the one who denies Jesus three times before the cock crows. What kind of performance review would you have given Peter? But notice how Jesus speaks to him in this passage:

> When Jesus came to the region of Caesarea Philippi, he asked his disciples, "Who do people say the Son of Man is?"
>
> They replied, "Some say John the Baptist; others say Elijah; and still others, Jeremiah or one of the prophets."
>
> "But what about you?" he asked. "Who do you say I am?"
>
> Simon Peter answered, "You are the Messiah, the Son of the living God."
>
> Jesus replied, "Blessed are you, Simon son of Jonah, for this was not revealed to you by flesh and blood, but by my Father in heaven. And I tell you that you are Peter, and on this rock I will build my church, and the gates of Hades will not overcome it. I will give you the keys of the kingdom of heaven; whatever you bind on earth will be bound in heaven, and whatever you loose on earth will be loosed in heaven." (Matthew 16:13-19)

This is a remarkable and public "performance review." Despite the many gaffes Peter had made previously, and those he would make after, on this occasion, when Peter correctly answers his question, Jesus is effusive in his praise. In front of the other disciples he elevates Peter and announces that he will become their eventual leader. Just imagine the wind this must have put in Peter's sails. In the years that would follow, Peter would be arrested, beaten, imprisoned, and persecuted as the leader of the early church. Ultimately, he died a martyr's death, brutally crucified upside down. I wonder how many times in the midst of these trials Peter found encouragement by thinking back to that singular moment when his Savior praised him and placed full confidence in him. I hope you find this encouraging too because your Savior also has full confidence in you. "Therefore, if anyone is in Christ, the new creation has come: The old has gone, the new is here!" (2 Corinthians 5:17).

Encouragement is free, it costs you nothing, but it will deliver a huge return on investment. And it works at all levels. You can encourage people below you, above you, and across from you in the organization. When your coworker in another department does something well, tell him how much you appreciate him. When your boss does something great, affirm her. As a leader, having encouraging people around me made a huge difference. My chief of staff at World Vision, Brian, was my Barnabas, the friend and traveling companion of Paul whose name in Scripture means "son of encouragement." Brian always believed in me, and his constant encouragement helped me accomplish much more than I could have ever done alone. People like that give you energy and confidence. Be one of them and surround yourself with people who are encouragers.

> **YOU CAN ENCOURAGE PEOPLE BELOW YOU, ABOVE YOU, AND ACROSS FROM YOU IN THE ORGANIZATION.**

18

PERSEVERANCE

HANG IN THERE

SCRIPTURE ➤ "Consider it pure joy, my brothers and sisters, whenever you face trials of many kinds, because you know that the testing of your faith produces perseverance. Let perseverance finish its work so that you may be mature and complete, not lacking anything." (James 1:2-4)

LEADERSHIP PRINCIPLE ➤ When a leader exhibits perseverance and grit in the face of difficult challenges, it sustains hope and lifts the confidence of their entire team.

Never give in. Never give in. Never, never, never, never—
in nothing, great or small, large or petty—never give
in, except to convictions of honor and good sense.

WINSTON CHURCHILL

I HAVE BEEN A SUCKER FOR all the Rocky movies over the years. There's something about Rocky Balboa that America loves. He's the quintessential underdog from South Philly. As a boxer, he doesn't have any of the dazzling moves or fancy footwork that Muhammed

Ali possessed. He's got zero pizzazz. Rocky's a plodder with little flair and average skills. But in every Rocky movie his flashier, more skilled opponents underestimate him. In the classic Rocky boxing match, he gets the daylights beat out of him for ten or twelve rounds. He gets knocked down over and over, but every time he's down—he manages to get back up. His eye's swollen shut and his face is a mask of blood, but he keeps coming at his opponent. He just never quits. And of course, in every movie Rocky somehow manages to prevail, not because he's a better boxer, but because he refuses to give up. Here's a quintessential Rocky quote from his 2006 sequel: "It ain't about how hard you hit. It's about how hard you can get hit and keep moving forward. . . . That's how winning is done!" Rocky won through sheer grit and perseverance. So, what does Rocky's philosophy of life have to do with leadership? It turns out that what made Rocky a successful boxer also makes for effective leaders.

One of the surprising findings documented in *Good to Great*, Jim Collins's watershed book on the best-performing American companies, was that the best leaders of the most successful companies in America were individuals characterized by two things: a blend of deep personal humility and intense professional will or perseverance. In describing these CEOs, he coined the phrase "Level 5 leaders." The Level 5 leaders he documented seemed to challenge the prevailing stereotypes of top-flight leaders in our culture. They were not the "bigger than life, take no prisoners" personalities with huge egos. Instead, they were typically quiet, reserved, and even introverted. But the two qualities that set them apart were a deep sense of personal humility—that it was not about them—and a dogged commitment to persevere in the face of challenges and adversity.

I've already spoken about the leadership quality of humility in chapter eight but would now like to speak to the value of perseverance in a leader. Perseverance, like most of the other leadership qualities I write about in this book, does not require a person to master any new skill set. It is not dependent on intelligence, creativity, or genius. It just requires a refusal to give up, no matter how hard the challenge.

Let me break down this leadership quality of perseverance into two categories: *Goal perseverance* is staying the course to accomplish something difficult. *Situational perseverance* is enduring a difficult situation in your life or work.

GOAL PERSEVERANCE

Leadership is about mobilizing groups of people to accomplish goals. Goal perseverance is about accomplishing something hard. Accomplishing easy things generally doesn't require much persistence. But when you set ambitious goals, they are going to be much harder to achieve, hence the need for stubborn perseverance. A leader who exhibits this kind of grit sets a positive example for their team members. It requires believing so passionately that something is possible that those around you start to believe it as well. That kind of belief and determination becomes contagious. Let me share an example.

I've already written about the commitment World Vision made to tackle the AIDS crisis in Africa. It was a daunting task fraught with risk that required the organization to confront terrible human suffering, loss, and grief. My smartest advisers believed it was "mission impossible" and urged me not to "go there." And in the early days I admit that it felt like an impossible mission.

I remember my first meeting with one of our high net-worth donors to ask him for financial support. After I described the devastation of AIDS and World Vision's plan to work in AIDS-ravaged communities in Africa, he stopped me and said he didn't want to talk about it, that it literally made him sick to think about AIDS, and that he would not donate his money to support our work with AIDS-affected communities. Wow! That's when I knew confronting AIDS would be an uphill battle.

To raise support and awareness, we took our message on the road on an eighteen-city speaking tour. In one of the early cities, Knoxville, Tennessee, I remember the discouragement I felt. We had planned a pastors' breakfast, believing we could attract more than one hundred pastors. We promoted it heavily in churches and on the radio. In addition to myself and a couple of other World Vision leaders, C. Everett Koop had agreed to speak at the event. He was the eminent former surgeon general who presided over the first AIDS cases in America during the Reagan administration. So we ordered a breakfast buffet for one hundred pastors, believing they would respond. But only *three* pastors showed up—three! It was devastating. The church leaders just didn't seem to care about the AIDS pandemic. Disheartened but undeterred, we conducted the event for just those three.

It would have been easy to cancel the rest of our tour and admit that this was a losing proposition. But the cause was far too important, and quitting was just not an option. So we prayed and we persevered. Subsequent cities gradually brought more promising turnouts, and by the time our tour got to Minneapolis months later, we somehow managed to get nine hundred people to turn out in the midst of a Minnesota snowstorm for an AIDS awareness dinner. The

Minneapolis Star Tribune was so surprised that nine hundred Minnesotan Christians would turn out for a dinner about AIDS that they ran the story on the front page the next day. Months later I learned that the *Star Tribune* article had started to circulate in the halls of Congress just as President Bush's AIDS relief plan for Africa (PEPFAR) was making its way to the floor for a vote. I was told that when some members of Congress, those who were on the fence, learned that nine hundred evangelicals in the heartland had braved a snowstorm because they were concerned about the impact of AIDS on African families, they decided to vote for the bill instead of against it. It passed in the House of Representatives 276 to 145 and was subsequently passed in the Senate and signed into law. Fifteen billion dollars was made available to help desperate men, women, and children around the world who had been victims of HIV/AIDS.

Despite the compelling biblical case for caring for widows and orphans in their distress, it was still hard to persuade American Christians and church leaders that the AIDS pandemic deserved their compassion and involvement. World Vision faced significant roadblocks and opposition from some key Christian leaders and denominational heads. But we refused to give up. We flew dozens of influential pastors and leaders to Africa to see for themselves what AIDS was doing to children and their families. We also asked our largest donors to come with us to witness firsthand the ravages of the pandemic.

Finding ways to communicate the scope and scale of the human tragedy that was taking place was critical. In one community in Zambia, we took a census and found that there were more than thirty-five hundred orphaned children in just that single village. I had their names typed and printed and I put them in a binder, which

I took with me when meeting with donors and church leaders. I asked them to leaf through the seventy-five pages and read some of the names. Then I told them there were thirteen million more orphans like these in Africa alone. A binder containing their names would require 275,000 pages! In my talks I painted a mental picture for my audience by asking them to imagine a line of orphaned children joining hands to form a human chain. And then I told them that this chain of orphans would crisscross America—shore to shore—some five and a half times. Then I asked if they would be willing to help.

The tide began to turn as more pastors and donors began to share our passion and commitment. Donations started to pour in from people who had heard and responded to our message, and slowly but surely attitudes began to change. We had consistently and passionately sounded the "fire alarm," and good-hearted pastors and Christians began to respond.

Like Paul, we believed God would give us the strength to persevere. We named our campaign the Hope Initiative, a fitting name that harks back to God's promise that perseverance produces hope: "And we boast in the hope of the glory of God. Not only so, but we also glory in our sufferings, because we know that suffering produces perseverance; perseverance, character; and character, hope. And hope does not put us to shame, because God's love has been poured out into our hearts through the Holy Spirit, who has been given to us" (Romans 5:2-5).

Over those years, World Vision's entire global organization responded with passion. While initially reluctant, enthusiasm and commitment grew as dozens of key leaders in the US and around the world embraced the cause and offered their own unique contributions and skill sets to the effort. The Hope Initiative changed World Vision.

When leaders persevere in the face of adversity, they create a culture of hope, a culture that invites people to see what's possible, a culture that believes a better future is attainable. And hope sustains people in the face of great adversity.

WHEN LEADERS PERSEVERE IN THE FACE OF ADVERSITY, THEY CREATE A CULTURE OF HOPE.

SITUATIONAL PERSEVERANCE

Situational perseverance (enduring difficult circumstances) is different from *goal* perseverance. Life is hard, and few of us will make it through life without facing a succession of challenging situations that will require endurance. Battling a disease, caring for an aging parent, raising a child with special needs, or losing a job are just a few examples.

And, in the course of your working life you will almost certainly find yourself in an unending series of work situations that will require perseverance: an unhealthy work culture, deep budget cuts in your department, being passed over for a promotion, working for a difficult boss, an economic downturn, an overwhelming workload, an ongoing problem with a coworker, or perhaps even a global pandemic that requires you to work from home and socially distance for months at a time. These situations will not only challenge your ability to endure but also test your Christian faith.

As a follower of Christ, how you respond to adversity is one of the major determinants of the effectiveness of your witness at work. Let me share one such story from my own career that you might relate to.

It's often been said that people don't quit their jobs, they quit their bosses. Working under a leader who is arrogant, manipulative, self-important, clueless, or just plain mean can be both emotionally and professionally traumatic. Sadly, I've had more than one bad boss during my career, and so will you. Surviving and even thriving under a difficult supervisor requires perseverance.

After I had been at Lenox for six years, the CEO who had hired me and with whom I had worked so well left the company. Over our years together he had promoted me several times—all the way to chief operating officer. When he left, I was hoping that this might be my big break and that I would be selected to replace him as president and CEO. But that was not in the cards. Instead, the chairman of Lenox's parent company decided to hire a new CEO externally. In other words, I got passed over. While I was, of course, disappointed, I determined to make the best of it by supporting the new leader.

Initially, everyone was hopeful that the new leader would be able to add real value and help take Lenox to the next level. But it only took a few weeks for people to realize that this was going to be a difficult ride. While he did bring some new perspectives and approaches to the company, the new CEO also had a volatile and intimidating leadership style. He often publicly reprimanded and embarrassed people during meetings. At times you could almost see the storm clouds gathering on his face before he lashed out angrily at someone. He could be cruel, manipulative, and self-serving. People began to fear their sessions with him.

On one occasion, he abruptly fired a lower-level staff member who had a family to support just because she had made a simple spelling error in a note that he had asked her to send out. He then called in that employee's division president and angrily berated him for allowing such incompetence in his organization. It was bad. People were fearful and discouraged. With a bit of black humor, some even started referring to him as "the prince of darkness."

Perhaps this situation sounds familiar to you. Over the course of your working life, you will inevitably encounter bosses or coworkers who are extremely difficult to work with. And surviving, let alone thriving, in such a situation will not be easy. My advice to you is simple. Stay positive. Do your best to embody values such as integrity, humility, humor, excellence, courage, love, and encouragement in your day-to-day interactions. Be helpful and keep your eye on the greater good. Even difficult bosses often respond positively to people who present themselves in this way. At the end of the day, you can only control your behavior, not theirs. And be patient, believing that your good behavior will make a positive difference. Here's what Paul urged us to do in the face of persecution: "Bless those who persecute you; bless and do not curse. . . . Do not repay anyone evil for evil. Be careful to do what is right in the eyes of everyone. If it is possible, as far as it depends on you, live at peace with everyone" (Romans 12:14, 17-18). You can be a peacemaker in the midst of a difficult situation.

My approach was to try to stay positive, making myself helpful and useful without embracing his negative leadership style. Because I had been at Lenox for years, I could be an interpreter and guide for him as he sought to understand a new industry and business. I tried to use humor to deflect some of his negative tendencies. The result was that we managed to maintain a fairly positive working relationship as he began to depend on me for advice and counsel.

These are also the times when you can shine as an ambassador for Christ. During that difficult season at Lenox, I did my best to help the organization cope by protecting people in meetings and trying to diffuse the CEO's mercurial outbursts. I tried to be a mediator on contentious issues, finding compromises that he would accept. I seemed to be able to find ways to calm him down and prevent meetings from getting ugly. In fact, it got to the point where some people only scheduled sessions with him if I could be in the room.

All of this helped us make the best out of a bad situation, but over time key people started to leave because the culture was so demoralizing. Finally, I lost one of my four talented division presidents and, just a few weeks later, I lost another. The organization was beginning to unravel. I thought about leaving myself but decided to stick it out, reasoning that maybe I could still salvage the situation. Jumping ship from a company I had invested years in just didn't feel right. And I believed that the parent company was beginning to become disenchanted with the CEO they had chosen.

About two and a half years in, we had a large, offsite strategy meeting with all the top executives from our parent company. On the first morning, while still in my hotel room, I received a 7:00 a.m. phone call from the chairman of the board. "Rich, will you come to my room at 7:30? I have an issue I need to discuss." Now, no one wants an early-morning phone call from the chairman demanding that they come to his hotel room. It was mildly terrifying.

When I arrived, he asked me to sit and abruptly told me that he had just accepted the CEO's resignation minutes before. Apparently, he had become increasingly aware of the turmoil at Lenox and the exodus of key leaders. Then he smiled and asked me if I would accept his offer to become the new CEO of Lenox. He observed that I had been faithful in many different roles within the company, that I had been patient, and that he now had confidence that I could do the job. My situational perseverance

> **A CHRISTIAN LEADER CAN BE AN ISLAND IN THE STORM FOR PEOPLE WHO ARE HURTING IN A DIFFICULT WORK ENVIRONMENT.**

had paid off. Just a few minutes later, we walked together into the leadership meeting, and he made the big announcement.

In the months leading up to this there had been some very dark times at work when I wondered whether I would even survive the toxic work environment. But those challenges also offered me the opportunity to shine some light into the darkness for others who were struggling. If our job as Christ's ambassadors involves being healers of the brokenness we find in our world, then crises become some of the best opportunities we have for our witness. A Christian leader can be an island in the storm for people who are hurting in a difficult work environment. If you can personally rise above the anxiety of a stressful situation with a spirit of peace, your steadiness can lift the spirits of those who are struggling. Hardship can provide a wonderful opportunity for you to demonstrate your faith by caring for others.

But let me be clear that perseverance must also have limits. If you are in a work situation where you are being continually abused or sexually harassed, or if you are being asked to do things that are unethical, perseverance is not the

> **HARDSHIP CAN PROVIDE A WONDERFUL OPPORTUNITY FOR YOU TO DEMONSTRATE YOUR FAITH BY CARING FOR OTHERS.**

proper response. In these cases, you should report the abuses appropriately, usually to the human resources department. If that isn't possible, you may need to get yourself out of the abusive situation. Some workplaces are just too toxic and dangerous to endure.

PAUL'S PERSEVERANCE

When we turn to Scripture, we see that perseverance was a core value that characterized the first-century church leaders as they

213

faced constant trials and persecution. Shockingly, eleven of the twelve disciples died violent deaths as martyrs for their faith. If you feel like you are facing tough challenges in your life or in your workplace, consider for a moment the hardships Paul described:

> I have worked much harder, been in prison more frequently, been flogged more severely, and been exposed to death again and again. Five times I received from the Jews the forty lashes minus one. Three times I was beaten with rods, once I was pelted with stones, three times I was shipwrecked, I spent a night and a day in the open sea, I have been constantly on the move. I have been in danger from rivers, in danger from bandits, in danger from my fellow Jews, in danger from Gentiles; in danger in the city, in danger in the country, in danger at sea; and in danger from false believers. I have labored and toiled and have often gone without sleep; I have known hunger and thirst and have often gone without food; I have been cold and naked. Besides everything else, I face daily the pressure of my concern for all the churches. Who is weak, and I do not feel weak? Who is led into sin, and I do not inwardly burn? (2 Corinthians 11:23-29)

I read this passage whenever I am feeling down about my own life challenges. It tends to put my small crises in perspective. Paul knew the meaning of perseverance. Yet in Philippians Paul tells us how he was able to bear these trials. "I know what it is to be in need, and I know what it is to have plenty. I have learned the secret of being content in any and every situation, whether well fed or hungry, whether living in plenty or in want. I can do all this through him who gives me strength" (Philippians 4:12-13).

YOUR PERSEVERANCE AS A LEADER CAN SUSTAIN HOPE AND LIFT THE SPIRITS OF YOUR ENTIRE TEAM IN THE MIDST OF TRIALS.

His secret was to trust God to give him the strength to endure. Paul knew that God's purposes for his life would prevail despite his trials—perhaps even because of his trials. Indeed, most of his New Testament letters were written during his imprisonments. In my situation at Lenox, my willingness to endure alongside my co-workers was only possible through him who gave me strength. Remember, your perseverance as a leader can sustain hope and lift the spirits of your entire team in the midst of trials.

19

LISTENING

BEES DO IT

SCRIPTURE ➤ "The way of a fool is right in his own eyes, but a wise man listens to advice." (Proverbs 12:15 ESV)

LEADERSHIP PRINCIPLE ➤ A leader who carefully and consistently listens to the people around them makes better decisions because each of those people is made in the image of God and has unique talents and insights to contribute.

When you talk, you are only repeating what you already know. But if you listen, you may learn something new.

DALAI LAMA

On August 28, 1963, during the historic March on Washington, Martin Luther King Jr. delivered one of the most famous and powerful speeches in American history. He had written out his text for the speech the night before, staying up until four in the morning working on it. But if you listen to recordings of this speech, toward the end before he launches into the rousing "I have a dream" refrain, there is a long pause. At that moment, when King looked at his notes, the next section of his remarks didn't feel right to him. And he paused for a full ten seconds, thinking about what he should say next. During that pause, gospel singer Mahalia Jackson, who was standing behind him, said, "Tell them about the dream, Martin, tell them about the dream!" King had used his "I have a dream" language in earlier speeches, but he had not planned to use it that day. But during that long, ten-second pause, as he wrestled with what to say next, he listened. Then he launched into the soaring prose that would make history on that hot summer day—all because he listened to another's voice.

Dr. King is often remembered as a solitary figure, a thundering prophet who seemed to single-handedly lead the civil rights movement in the fifties and sixties. But one of the qualities that made him a great leader was his willingness to listen to the counsel of others. Here is what journalist John Blake wrote about King's leadership style:

> Even King's management style was built on listening. He surrounded himself with a team of rivals who constantly battled one another in the Southern Christian Leadership Conference, the civil rights group King co-founded. Several openly challenged or disagreed with King—and that's exactly what he wanted, says Andrew Young, the former United Nations Ambassador who was part of King's inner circle.
>
> "The SCLC was always a battle of egos," Young said in the landmark "Eyes on a Prize" civil rights documentary. "We were like a team of wild horses. Each one had very strong opinions and their own ideas about the way the movement should go, and Dr. King encouraged that. And our meetings were loud and raucous and he quietly sat by until we fought issues out, and then he would usually decide."

Dr. King led one of the most controversial and contentious movements in American history, a movement that included many strong voices, personalities, and opinions. But instead of going it alone and doing it "his way," King listened to the counsel of many before deciding how he would lead.

As I stated in chapter eight, leaders too often believe their own press clippings. They reason that they have become the leader because they are smarter, better, and more capable than the people around them. And so they often choose to follow their own intuition and make decisions without the benefit of counsel and input from others. The Bible has a quite a few pointed things to say about such people, but Proverbs 12:15 is a good summary: "Fools think their own way is right, but the wise listen to advice" (NRSV). In other words, a leader who doesn't listen is a fool.

The best leaders are good listeners. Good listeners benefit from hearing different opinions, gaining new insights, and getting feedback on their ideas and instincts. The more information they gather, the better the decisions they ultimately make. This is reason enough to become a good listener, but for the Christian leader, as I have already argued, there is another truth that is profound: the people around you are made in the image of God, each uniquely endowed with specific gifts and abilities that are different from your own. As C. S. Lewis once said: "There are no ordinary people. You have never talked to a mere mortal." The leader who recognizes this and listens to others draws from a divine well and will always have an edge over a leader who does not.

GOOD LISTENERS BENEFIT FROM HEARING DIFFERENT OPINIONS, GAINING NEW INSIGHTS, AND GETTING FEEDBACK ON THEIR IDEAS AND INSTINCTS.

THE WAGGLE DANCE

Having a degree in neurobiology and animal behavior has rarely come in handy over my management career. However, there is one remarkable animal behavior that has stuck with me over the years. It is the process by which honeybees make collective decisions. You heard me correctly: honeybees collaborate in decision making.

Biologist Karl von Frisch discovered that honeybees can communicate with other members of the hive through a kind of dance. This "waggle dance" allows them to share information with each other about the direction and distance to water sources, patches of flowers yielding nectar and pollen, or a potential new nest location.

Let's say the hive needs to find a new location for their nest. When one bee has discovered a possible new nesting site, it returns to the hive and performs a waggle dance for the other bees that pinpoints that location's direction and distance—almost like GPS coordinates. The other bees then fly to that location to see for themselves. At the start of this consultation process there may be five or six possible locations, each being communicated by different bees as if to say to the others, "Hey, here's what I think." More bees dutifully fly to check out the possible sites and return to the nest to dance their agreement or disagreement with each location. Gradually, through this iterative "listening" process, consensus is reached as the consultation process begins to narrow the choices to two or three, each bee contributing their "opinion" of each possible nesting site. Once more than 50 percent of the bees coalesce around one of the sites, the decision is made, and the entire swarm of bees suddenly and decisively flies to the new destination. (Yes, there really is an amazing Creator God in heaven!) This honeybee decision-making process models a kind of iterative democratic model for decision making that aggregates the wisdom of all the members of the hive.

THE WAGGLE AT WORLD VISION

Okay, so how does this relate to hives of humans? A few years into my tenure at World Vision I felt that a significant reorganization of the various functions needed to happen. As CEO I could have sequestered myself in a conference room with my human resources leader and, like Moses, just come down from "Mount Sinai" with the new structure chiseled on a couple of stone tablets. But because World Vision's culture had a strong expectation of collaborative decision making, I took a different approach. Over a period of weeks, I held roughly thirty one-on-one discussions with leaders from multiple levels and departments to ask for their ideas and input. I then held a series of broader town halls to bounce ideas around and solicit further input. I also spoke with my board members.

As I moved closer to making the final decision, I brought together about twenty-five key leaders for a full-day session. I divided them into about five or six small cross-functional groups, and I asked each group to pretend that the final decision was theirs and instructed them to create their recommended organizational structure. Then the groups were to come back together to present their solutions to the larger group complete with their rationale. I emphasized that they needed to work together without regard to rank or departmental loyalties because we were seeking the best solution for the entire organization.

After a few hours all the teams came back together, each excited about their group's solution. The good news was that after all this work and "waggling," the "bees" were coalescing around a few strong themes and concepts. When we were done, I thanked everyone for their good work and told them that I would take each of their designs into consideration. Then I did sequester myself in a room with the head of human resources to review all the input we had received. Using that input, we created our new organizational structure. The following week we announced it and began rolling it out.

I took some risks in using this kind of transparent process, but it paid off. The new structure was widely embraced with very little controversy. Lots of people had been involved, and most of them could see some of their thinking represented in the new structure. People were encouraged that their leader had honestly cared about their opinions and had taken the time to listen. That listening not only had resulted in a better decision but had also created a ground-swell of acceptance and good will. The hive was happy.

THE WISDOM OF THE CROWD

One of the most compelling books I have read related to the importance of soliciting input from others in decision making is *The Wisdom of Crowds* by James Surowiecki. It speaks to the almost uncanny ability of a group of ordinary people to solve complex problems more effectively than the "experts." The "crowd" almost always outperforms the solitary expert.

The book opens with an anecdote about an eighty-five-year-old British scientist, Francis Galton, strolling through a county fair in England in 1906. Galton happened upon a weight-judging exhibit where fairgoers could buy a ticket and guess the weight of an ox to be later slaughtered and butchered. The closest guessers would win prizes. Galton's hypothesis was that not many would come close to the right answer, save a few of the real "experts" in the crowd—people who were livestock owners or butchers themselves with years of experience. Afterwards, Galton was given the tickets containing the roughly eight hundred guesses to analyze. To his astonishment, while no one guessed the exact weight of the ox correctly, the average of the eight hundred guesses came out to 1,197 pounds. The actual correct weight was 1,198 pounds! The crowd's guess was nearly perfect and better than any of the individual experts within the group.

Surowiecki then spends the next 270 pages demonstrating that the "wisdom" found in these kinds of collective judgments has been replicated and validated across a wide variety of fields of endeavor and complex situations. He states his thesis thusly: "The powerful truth is that . . . under the right circumstances, groups are remarkably intelligent, and are often smarter than the smartest people in them." This empirical truth reinforces the Christian view of the unique giftedness of each person. Paul recognized the collective talents of a group of individuals in describing the church: "Now to each one the manifestation of the Spirit is given for the common good. . . . God has placed the parts in the body, every one of them, just as he wanted them to be. If they were all one part, where would the body be? As it is, there are many parts, but one body. . . . Now you are the body of Christ, and each one of you is a part of it" (1 Corinthians 12:7, 18-20, 27).

While a secular organization is not the same as the church, the principle holds; the people you work with are each uniquely endowed by their Creator in specific ways. Each one of them has a unique contribution, insight, and perspective to contribute to decision making. This is one of those rare leadership "ahas"! When you as a leader engage a group of individuals to tackle a particular problem, or decide on a specific course of action,

THE COLLECTIVE WISDOM OF THE GROUP WILL ALMOST ALWAYS BE BETTER THAN YOUR OWN PERSONAL INSTINCTS.

the collective wisdom of the group will almost always be better than your own personal instincts. At the very least, the collective wisdom will always be worth considering.

DIVERSITY IMPROVES THE CROWD'S WISDOM

One of Surowiecki's other key findings was that groups composed of more diverse individuals with different backgrounds made better decisions than more homogenous groups. This is also profound. Think about why. People with different backgrounds and life experiences have different insights and perspectives. When these different perspectives are expressed and considered, the multiple new data points contribute to making superior decisions. Diversity is desirable across multiple dimensions: gender, age, race, culture, education, geography, field of expertise, religion, and so on. Consistently listening to the ideas and insights of other people, especially people who are different than we are, results in better decisions. It gets us out of the "echo chamber" of homogeneity. Diversity in an organization should not be seen as some box-checking requirement imposed by human resources; it should be aggressively pursued as a vital competitive edge that enhances performance.

At Lenox, when we started listening to young brides and their mothers instead of our all-male product designers with degrees in art, our new designs started to sell and our market share soared. At Parker Brothers Games we brought in real kids to try our new games, believing that their insights might be better than those of our middle-aged product-development group. World Vision experienced explosive growth in the eighties and nineties when they put indigenous national leaders in charge of the work in their own countries and removed from leadership the mostly white, male, northern expats from the US, Canada, Europe, and Australia. At my first global World Vision leadership meeting in 1998, tears came to my eyes as four hundred people from almost one hundred countries sang "Great Is Thy Faithfulness" together, each in our native tongue. Today, the World Vision International board of directors is made up of twenty-four men and women from nineteen different countries. When that board meets, the richness of God's kingdom is represented

IF YOUR MINISTRY, COMPANY, SCHOOL, ORGANIZATION, OR TEAM LACKS DIVERSITY, YOU'RE OPERATING WITH A SERIOUS DISADVANTAGE.

around the table. If your ministry, company, school organization, or team lacks diversity, you're operating with a serious disadvantage.

BLACK AND WHITE AND GRAY

This unattributed quote captures a truth that is important for leaders to understand: "Don't define your world in black and white, because there is so much hiding amongst the grays." It has been my experience that most leadership decisions aren't black or white issues; they almost always present themselves in shades of gray. Which candidate should I hire, who should I promote, how should I

THE LEADER'S JOB IS TO FIND CLARITY IN THE MIDST OF THE GRAYNESS.

structure my group, how should we respond to a competitor's threat? There usually aren't simple answers to questions like these. In many decisions, the leader's task is to seek more certainty, and hopefully some consensus, by moving a 50/50 decision toward 60/40 or 70/30. The leader's job is to find clarity in the midst of the grayness, and that process is best done through careful listening.

Everyone knows the familiar phrase, "It's lonely at the top." But it doesn't need to be lonely. God has surrounded us with other people—not "mere mortals," as Lewis said, but people made in the image of God. And when we respect them, when we listen to them, when we invite them into the grayness with us, they can help us to become better leaders. And when you truly listen to others and show that you value their ideas and insights, you get another bonus—they feel affirmed and respected. Team members who feel affirmed and respected care more, work harder, and are more committed. There's that encouragement thing again. I said in chapter eight that a leader should surround themselves with smart, capable people and then give them permission to speak the truth to them. When you do this, and when you carefully listen to others, you gain access to the divine imprint God has placed within each person.

TAKING GOD TO WORK

20

SCRIPTURE ➤ "Peace be with you! As the Father has sent me, I am sending you." (John 20:21)

LEADERSHIP PRINCIPLE ➤ Success is not your goal. Faithfulness to God is your goal. For the Christian leader, faithfulness is success.

As Christians, we wake up each morning as those who are baptized. We are united with Christ and the approval of the Father is spoken over us. We are marked from our first waking moment by an identity that is given to us by grace: an identity that is deeper and more real than any identity we will don that day.

TISH HARRISON WARREN

Our spiritual lives cannot be measured by success as the world measures it, but only by what God pours through us—and we cannot measure that at all.

OSWALD CHAMBERS

TOMORROW, OR MAYBE MONDAY, most of you who are reading this book will go back to work. You may be returning to a job you love, to work with people you greatly admire, or you may be dreading yet another day in an unpleasant job in a toxic and demoralizing work environment. You might be incredibly successful in your chosen career, earning both recognition and great financial rewards, or you may be trapped in a dead-end job, underappreciated and with little to show for your efforts. Either way, God wants you to take your faith to work.

I imagine that if you've read this far you are likely someone who has leadership responsibilities and is seriously seeking to become a better leader—a Christian leader, a leader after God's own heart. You've probably felt uncertain about how your faith should play itself out at work. You have one foot planted in God's Word and the other planted in the working world, and there is tension between those two realities.

I began this book with the Scripture verse that totally changed my perspective on my work and my calling: "We are therefore Christ's ambassadors, as though God were making his appeal through us" (2 Corinthians 5:20). The remarkable truth that God has anointed us to be his ambassadors and has sent us into the world with that title and responsibility changes everything once we understand it. It means that our work is no longer merely the thing that we must do to earn money, nor is it just a vehicle for achieving professional success. It is no longer the place where we leave our faith at the door only to pick it up when we leave at the end of the day, and it is no longer the setting where we spend forty or fifty hours each week striving to achieve things that have no connection to our Christian faith and calling. No, our workplace is where we have been deliberately deployed by God; it's the place he has called us, sent us, and commissioned us as Christ's ambassadors.

Just after his resurrection, Jesus appeared to his disciples and reminded them of their purpose: "As the Father has sent me, I am sending you" (John 20:21). Just as they were sent into the world by Jesus to live lives transformed by the gospel, you also have been sent. The day you accepted Jesus Christ as your Lord and Savior you were repurposed. You were given a new vocation, a new identity. And your workplace and your community

WE ARE TO BE THE TANGIBLE DEMONSTRATION OF THE LOVE, CHARACTER, AND TRUTH OF CHRIST AS WE LIVE OUT OUR FAITH IN A VERY PUBLIC WAY.

became the mission fields where you live out that vocation and identity. You have been sent there to shine your light into the darkness.

But just what does it mean to take God to work with us? What does that new vocation entail? As Christ's ambassadors we are called to embody the values and character of the one who sent us. We are to be the tangible demonstration of the love, character, and truth of Christ as we live out our faith in a very public way. Living out your faith doesn't require you to evangelize everyone at work or lead a Bible study during your lunch hour. It's more about being than doing—being that light in the darkness as you reflect the character of Christ through your daily work. The love of Christ in us should overflow into our workplaces and communities. And, as I have argued in these pages, our light shines brightest when we embrace and display the values of Christ's coming kingdom: things like integrity, excellence, courage, love, humility, encouragement, perseverance, generosity, and forgiveness—Christ shining through us.

When we do this consistently, we stand out, we set ourselves apart, and we provoke the question to which Christ is the answer. That's what our ambassador status looks like in practice.

"But," you say, "what about the pressures at work to conform, succeed, and deliver results? If I really stand up for these values I'll be the odd man out. I won't fit in to the culture where I work." As an ambassador for Christ, the hope is that you *will* stand out rather than fit in. Your values *will* set you apart as you become a trusted colleague, a voice of reason, a pillar of integrity, a giver of encouragement, and a source of compassion for your coworkers. And this means that you must march to a different drummer.

OUR LIGHT SHINES BRIGHTEST WHEN WE EMBRACE AND DISPLAY THE VALUES OF CHRIST'S COMING KINGDOM.

Instead of being motivated by money, title, politics, and ambition, you are there to be the "fragrance" of Christ, as Paul says, "For we are to God the fragrance of Christ among those who are being saved and among those who are perishing" (2 Corinthians 2:15 NKJV).

THE IDOL OF SUCCESS

I need to speak one last time about the subtle allure of success in our culture because I am certain that just about everyone reading this book wants to be successful. I made the provocative statement at the beginning of this book that success should not be our goal, which I realize runs contrary to just about everything we are told. The world we live in glorifies and celebrates success in all fields of endeavor. The places where we work measure and expect successful outcomes from us. We are all immersed in a success culture defined by some combination of achievement, money, power, and status. And, if we are honest with ourselves, most of us are drinking some of the success Kool-Aid that's being served up. We even pass it on to our children as we set expectations for their performance at school, in sports, and in their future college and career choices. The "gospel of success" is everywhere.

But then comes Mother Teresa's remarkable statement: "God did not call me to be successful, he called me to be faithful." *Faithful, not successful* was her mantra. With that statement, Mother Teresa redefined success—she turned it inside out. Because, for a follower of Christ, faithfulness is success, and success is faithfulness.

Don't misunderstand me. Being successful in the conventional sense of the word is not a bad thing, it's just not the main thing. It's normal for us to want our children to do well and to realize their full, God-given potential. It's okay if all our effort and hard work result in financial and professional success. In fact, if you practice the values set forth in this book (and in Scripture) you will increase your likelihood of professional and financial success. Success may be a byproduct of your faithfulness, but don't make it your reason for living.

> **SUCCESS MAY BE A BYPRODUCT OF YOUR FAITHFULNESS, BUT DON'T MAKE IT YOUR REASON FOR LIVING.**

As Scripture warns us, "Those who want to get rich fall into temptation and a trap and into many foolish and harmful desires that plunge people into ruin and destruction" (1 Timothy 6:9).

CHASING AFTER THE WIND

King Solomon understood worldly success. He was number one on the "Forbes 400 wealthiest people" list of his time—maybe of all time. He was the ruler over the United Kingdom of Israel and had a reputation for being the wisest man in the world. Other rulers came to Solomon to seek his advice and his favor. And Solomon denied himself no indulgence or pleasure. He writes about his achievements in the book of Ecclesiastes:

> I undertook great projects: I built houses for myself and planted vineyards. I made gardens and parks and planted all kinds of fruit trees in them. I made reservoirs to water groves of flourishing trees. I bought male and female slaves and had other slaves who were born in my house. I also owned more herds and flocks than anyone in Jerusalem before me. I amassed silver and gold for myself, and the treasure of kings and provinces. I acquired male and female singers, and a harem as well—the delights of a man's heart. I became greater by far than anyone in Jerusalem before me. In all this my wisdom stayed with me.
>
> I denied myself nothing my eyes desired;
> I refused my heart no pleasure.
> My heart took delight in all my labor,
> and this was the reward for all my toil. (Ecclesiastes 2:4-10)

You would think that Solomon, of all people, would celebrate all that he had accomplished with great satisfaction, but no.

> Yet when I surveyed all that my hands had done
> and what I had toiled to achieve,
> everything was meaningless, a chasing after the wind;
> nothing was gained under the sun. (Ecclesiastes 2:11)

When Solomon looked back on his life and assessed his unfathomable success, this was his bottom line: "meaningless, a chasing after the wind." Over twelve chapters Solomon continues his withering argument that, in the end, all his striving and achievement, all his success, had really amounted to nothing. Then, in the very last verses of the book, he pronounces his conclusion. If success is meaningless, then what is the purpose of our lives?

Now all has been heard;
  here is the conclusion of the matter:
Fear God and keep his commandments,
  for this is the duty of all mankind.
For God will bring every deed into judgment,
  including every hidden thing,
  whether it is good or evil. (Ecclesiastes 12:13-14)

The true purpose of every human being is to "fear God and keep his commandments." Solomon was essentially paraphrasing the answer to my old Catholic catechism question: "Why did God make you? God made you to know him, to love him, and to serve him in this life." And Solomon was also channeling Mother Teresa: "God did not call me to be successful, he called me to be faithful."

You see, it's only when we are able to redefine what success means in our faith walk and close our ears to the chants of our culture that we can begin to live into the higher calling of our lives and our work, to be those "ambassadors" for Christ. Then we can get out of the rat race of success, off the treadmill of performance, and set our eyes on a different prize. "Brothers and sisters, I do not consider myself yet to have taken hold of it. But one thing I do: Forgetting what is behind and straining toward what is ahead, I press on toward the goal to win the prize for which God has called me heavenward in Christ Jesus" (Philippians 3:13-14).

Yes, we are to work with excellence and diligence wherever we serve, not because *success* is our goal but because *faithfulness* is our goal. When good ambassadors demonstrate excellence, they enhance the reputation of the one they represent. And that excellence, when combined with courage, humility, forgiveness, encouragement, generosity, and the other godly characteristics of our life in Christ,

233

will be attractive and compelling to a watching world. We will become the transformative salt and light that Jesus spoke of: "You are the light of the world. A town built on a hill cannot be hidden. Neither do people light a lamp and put it under a bowl. Instead they put it on its stand, and it gives light to everyone in the house. In the same way, let your light shine before others, that they may see your good deeds and glorify your Father in heaven" (Matthew 5:14-16).

BROKEN VESSELS

One of the remarkable truths about our faith is that God has chosen to use us, flawed as we are. He could have chosen to intervene in our world more directly. But instead he invited us to participate in his great revolution to change the world. He has called us to be his transformed people engaged in transforming the world, making it more pleasing to him, even though we do it as broken vessels, "jars of clay," with all our cracks and flaws on display. "But we have this treasure in jars of clay to show that this all-surpassing power is from God and not from us" (2 Corinthians 4:7).

As Christ's ambassadors, most of us leave much to be desired. In our service to the Lord we go through crises, we make mistakes, we suffer setbacks—and if we're human, we experience failures. But despite all of this we can still trust that God is using us—warts and all. Faithful, not successful, is what he asks. And faithful doesn't mean

HE HAS CALLED US TO BE HIS TRANSFORMED PEOPLE ENGAGED IN TRANSFORMING THE WORLD.

perfect but simply that we keep trying, keep picking ourselves up when we stumble, and remain committed to being his disciples no matter what.

The Bible is filled with flawed leaders who had massive spiritual failings: David, who sinned with Bathsheba; Peter, who denied the Lord three times; Moses, who whined about God's command to confront Pharaoh; Abraham, who lied over and over again about his wife, Sarah; Jacob, who was a deceptive manipulator for most of his life. But God used them anyway. And God can use you too, even when you doubt you are making a difference. If you are that person who sometimes feels like a failure in your Christian walk, and if you doubt that God can use you, I have this one last precious encouragement for you. So please listen.

What God is accomplishing through you involves you, but it does not depend on you.

Abraham, at one hundred, was involved in God's promise of a son—but it did not depend on Abraham.

Moses was involved in confronting Pharaoh and leading God's people to the Promised Land, but it did not depend on Moses.

David and his sling were involved in slaying Goliath, but it did not depend on David.

Peter was involved in leading the first-century church, but it did not depend on Peter.

You see, in every case, the outcomes were delivered by God. These people were simply faithful leaders—not perfectly faithful by any means—and God used them to accomplish his purposes. And if you are faithful, God will use you to ac-

WHAT GOD IS ACCOMPLISHING THROUGH YOU INVOLVES YOU, BUT IT DOES NOT DEPEND ON YOU.

complish great things too—even when your impact seems insignificant and you can't see any positive outcomes from your witness. Even when you feel like a failure, God is working through you.

A PICTURE OF FAITHFULNESS

Merold Stern, the pastor who performed our marriage ceremony just after Reneé and I graduated from college, and his wife, Margaret, had a deep influence on our lives. Merold served most of his life as the pastor of a small, college-town church in Ithaca, New York. He preached faithfully every Sunday, counseled hundreds of students (like me), oversaw most of the church committees, and even sang in the choir on Sundays with his wife. Working quietly behind the scenes, Margaret was her own spiritual force, supporting Merold and their church with her gifts of hospitality and encouragement: putting on soup lunches and church dinners, managing daily vacation Bible school treats, and regularly hosting guests at teas and meals. Merold and Margaret served like that for some fifty years in a small church where weekly attendance ranged from fifty to a couple hundred, depending on the season. Merold never published a book, never appeared on the cover of *Christianity Today*, and never knew the limelight enjoyed by megachurch pastors whose names are nationally known. Margaret received even less recognition. Merold and Margaret, now in their nineties, are humble people of great wisdom and godliness.

I am sure that Merold sometimes felt like he wasn't having much impact for Christ—at least not compared to some of the Christian superstars of national prominence. But, you see, Merold and his indispensable partner, Margaret, were faithful with what God had given them to do, even though they may not have imagined the full influence of their ministry. We don't always see the ways God is working through us.

Jesus compares the growth of the kingdom of God to the germination of a seed: "This is what the kingdom of God is like. A man scatters seed on the ground. Night and day, whether he sleeps or gets up, the seed sprouts and grows, *though he does not know how.* All by itself the soil produces grain—first the stalk, then the head, then the full kernel in the head. As soon as the grain is ripe, he puts the sickle to it, because the harvest has come" (Mark 4:26-29). In other words, the farmer faithfully does his work, but he really has no understanding of just how God will ultimately transform his efforts into a harvest. The real magic happens after the seeds have been scattered. Our job, like the farmer's, is to faithfully scatter those seeds as we represent Christ, but it is God who ultimately brings the harvest. And the real harvest is something we may never see, as God works in the lives of the people we interact with every day.

Merold and Margaret impacted the lives of hundreds, maybe thousands, of Cornell students over fifty years. Their counseling, modeling, and mentorship deeply affected my and Reneé's commitment to Christ, and I know it impacted others in the same way. And the many students their ministry touched graduated and went on to become pastors, professors, business leaders, doctors, missionaries, and ministry heads who in turn influenced thousands and even millions of others in the course of their lives and careers. That is the true harvest God brought about from the seeds Merold and Margaret Stern so faithfully planted. They scattered the seeds, but God produced the harvest.

A SEED THAT BECAME AN ARCHBISHOP

I witnessed another stunning example of how God works miracles through the faithfulness of ordinary people when I met one of World Vision's former sponsored children in Kenya in 2017. In World Vision's ministry, several million children are currently sponsored, mostly by Christian families who are putting their faith into action by trying to help one child living in poverty. These families contribute a little more than a dollar a day, and World Vision uses those funds to help the children and their communities with clean water, education, improved health, better nutrition, and economic opportunities. The families that sponsor these kids are planting some critical seeds, but it is God who then uses these seeds to produce the true harvest that those families may never see. What do those children become? Who do they influence in the future, and what does that ripple effect look like five, twenty-five, or even a hundred years from now? A family that gives a few dollars a week to help a child has no idea how God might multiply their faithfulness.

On my trip to Kenya I was excited to meet this grown man named Jackson who had been sponsored way back in the 1970s. As a child he had lost his father, and his family had struggled in terrible poverty. But because of the faithful family that sponsored him, World Vision was able to bring help. Jackson now had food to eat, stayed healthy, went to World Vision's summer Bible programs, and was able to finish high school—quite an achievement back then. The family that had sponsored him was just trying to be faithful to God by helping one little boy living in poverty. And when Jackson turned eighteen, his sponsorship ended, and their job was done. But the true harvest came forty years later!

In 2016 that "little boy," Jackson Ole Sapit, was installed as the sixth archbishop of the Anglican Church of Kenya, responsible for the spiritual leadership of more than five million people in his country. The family that sponsored him was being faithful in a small thing, planting a few tiny seeds, but God was doing a big thing—he was growing an archbishop.

GOD'S LOVE LETTER TO THE WORLD

I began this book with the inspiring words of Mother Teresa, and it seems appropriate to end it with her words as well. During her remarkable life she traveled the world and met with presidents, prime ministers, and kings to advocate on behalf of the poor. She experienced global fame and recognition for her work. Mother Teresa was an amazing leader. But as extraordinary as her decades of leadership and faithful service to the poor were, she never saw greatness in herself. She knew where true greatness lay—in the hands of God—and she understood that what God was doing through her involved her but did not depend on her.

In 1946, while riding on a train from Calcutta to a retreat in the Himalayan foothills, she believed that she heard Jesus speak to her, calling her to serve the poor in Calcutta. These are the words she heard: "I want Indian Nuns, Missionaries of Charity, who would be my fire of love amongst the poor, the sick, the dying and the little children. *You are, I know, the most incapable person, weak and sinful, but just because you are that, I want to use you for my glory.* Wilt thou refuse?" She didn't refuse. She understood from the beginning that what God was doing through her depended on God and not her; God had told her so. She just needed to be faithful. Later in her life she captured this understanding of her relationship with God in a beautiful metaphor: "I'm a little pencil in the hand of a writing God, who is sending a love letter to the world." She saw herself as just "a little pencil" in the hand of God, a humble tool for God to use as he pleased. Isn't that a beautiful image? God is the author who is expressing his love for people all across the world. And when we make ourselves fully available to him, he uses us as "little pencils" to write those life-changing love letters. We become his messengers.

So, when you go to work tomorrow—or to that church committee meeting—or to that neighborhood gathering—just be that little pencil, surrendered and available to God. He has invited you to join him—to be his ambassador. He wants to use leaders like you to build for his kingdom—to demonstrate his love and character to a watching world—and to model a different way of living, working, and leading. God is calling you to be that kind of leader.

Because leadership matters to God.

POSTSCRIPT

As I was finishing this book, the twin pandemics of coronavirus and racial discrimination began raging across our country and the world, stopping all of us in our tracks. Never before in world history have there been crises that literally impacted every nation, institution, and person on the planet simultaneously. And as I finish this book, we still don't know what our collective future will look like.

But these crises have offered us a graduate-level course in leadership. I have watched as every leader in every institution in every sector of society has been confronted with the challenge of leading their people through these unprecedented times. Leaders of corporations, police forces, hospitals, churches, ministries, schools, nonprofits, community groups, small businesses, and governments have all been faced with excruciating choices and challenges. And these crises have revealed something about those leaders: the values on which their leadership is based. Because crises always reveal character.

Some leaders have risen to the challenge, demonstrating courage, vision, excellence, perseverance, sacrifice, empathy, integrity, encouragement, and humility. These leaders have put people first, fought for the greater good, and been sources of comfort, hope, and inspiration for the people in their care. Other leaders have instead acted in their own self-interest, protecting profits over people, placing blame on others, dividing instead of uniting, and letting political calculations supersede the real and desperate needs of people. Two kinds of leaders, two contrasting responses.

Jesus spoke to these foundational issues in the parable of the wise and foolish builders.

> Therefore, everyone who hears these words of mine and puts them into practice is like a wise man who built his house on the rock. The rain came down, the streams rose, and the winds blew and beat against that house; yet it did not fall, because it had its foundation on the rock. But everyone who hears these words of mine and does not put them into practice is like a foolish man who built his house on sand. The rain came down, the streams rose, and the winds blew and beat against that house, and it fell with a great crash. (Matthew 7:24-27)

The message of this book is about hearing Jesus' words and putting them into practice in your workplace. It's about building your career and your life on a foundation of rock, not sand, because over the course of your life and leadership, the rain *will* come down, the streams *will* rise, and the winds *will* blow. You will be challenged to lead through many such crises. The wise leader, the godly leader, the values-driven leader, will build their house on the rock—and they will not fall.

ACKNOWLEDGMENTS

IT IS CUSTOMARY in these acknowledgment pages to list the many people who have helped the author develop and write his or her book, and I have done that in my previous publishing ventures. As I'm now retired, this book was mostly a solo effort. But I do want to thank my editor, Ed Gilbreath, for recognizing the value of this message and advocating for IVP to publish it. And I appreciate the entire IVP team who helped me get this book across the finish line. Jeff Crosby, the publisher of IVP, clinched the deal by explaining to me that IVP was a "message publisher" rather than an "opportunity publisher"—meaning that their first priority was to publish books with important messages rather than looking first at the "celebrity" of the author, which is usually correlated with the volume of sales. Perhaps that's why I have read and cherished so many IVP books over the years, because they contained truly important messages for people seeking to become better disciples of Christ.

But the content of this book owes its greatest debt to the many colleagues and mentors who I have had the privilege of knowing and working with over the years. As I said in dedicating this book to them, these colleagues often modeled the seventeen values I chose to write about. Their positive examples shaped and inspired me as a leader. Some excelled in encouragement, some in vision or courage or humility, and others in perseverance, surrender, or excellence. They were people above me in the organization and also below me, because these values don't depend on one's rank. And some of them were people from other organizations whose leadership inspired me.

At the terrible risk of leaving some wonderful friends and colleagues out, I want to use this opportunity to name some of those who inspired me along the way and who brought such positive energy to the places where they worked. Here, in no particular order, is my list of heroes: Larry Probus, Bill Bracy, Charles Owubah, Ken Casey, Joyce Godwin, Steve Hayner, Edgar Sandoval, Dave Toycen, Connie Lenneberg, Jim Chiles, Brian Sytsma, Dave Herman, Atul Tandon, Joan Mussa, Bruce Wilkinson, Doug Treff, Jim Bere, John Crosby, Julie Regnier, Chris Glynn, Sam Jackson, Jon Warren, Marilee Dunker, Leighton Ford, Kari Costanza, Shelley Liester, Peter Gruol, Joanna Mockler, Joan Singleton, Cara Berggren, Rob Moll, Leith Anderson, Dan Hussar, Bob Snyder, Tom Costanza, Ed Radding, Jerry White, Horace Smith, Dolphus Weary, Marty Lonsdale, Corina Villacorta, Tami Heim, Tim Dearborn, Rudo Karambo, Michael Chitwood, Emmanuel Opong, Amanda Bowman, Jim Wallis, Jim Daly, Tim Costello, Jayakumar Christian, Wayne Parchman, Bobby Majka, Martha Curren, Bill Bryce, Ron Sider, Michael Messenger, Jim Lee, Donna Bunn, Dave Robinson, Brian Duss, Hoseung Yang, Chris Clarke, Thomas Chan, Bill Haslam, Kevin Chu, Paul Nelson, Rob Stevenson, Phil Orbanes, Mike Tracy, Chris Shore, Thomas Jenkins, Dana Buck, Lloyd Reeb, Clint Dougan, Manfred Grellert, Trihadi Saptoadi, Keith Stewart, Kathryn Compton, Torrey Olsen, Dan Martin, Andrea Schutz, Charlie Keith, John Makoni, Valdir Steurnagel, Princess Kasune Zulu, Bob Kelsey, Bob Flannery,

Sean Kerrigan, Margaret Schuler, Kathy Evans, Bob Zachritz, Roberta Hestenes, Amy Thompson, Jane Sutton-Redner, Christo Greyling, Stan Krangel, Christine Talbot, Tim Andrews, Steve Dill, Vinh Chung, Dan Busby, Kathy Currie, Jonathan Reckford, Andrew Morley, Gary Haugen, Max Lucado, Edgar Flores, Kent Hill, Steve Haas, Martha Curren, Bob Israel, Scott Jackson, Gary Duim, Wilfred Mlay, Stephen Lockley, Ray Norman, Brady Anderson, Scott Chin, Tim Carder, Rhea Goldman, Dave Mitchell, Jim Solomon, Milana McLead, Jo Anne Lyons, John Thomas, John Clause, Joe Riverson, Les Kline, Lisa Archambault, Mike Mantel, Lou Fantin, Sam Kameleson, and Bismark Nerquaye-Tetteh.

I ask forgiveness for my imperfect memory in inevitably leaving some great colleagues out, but I felt it was important for me to thank and acknowledge some of the many people who brought richness and joy to my leadership journey. Finally, I am grateful to my wife, Reneé, who is my constant sounding board and editor in all things. She walked with me through the ups and downs of a forty-four year career with amazing patience, grace, understanding, encouragement, and advice.

NOTES

INTRODUCTION

3   *My dear Senator*: Quoted in Phyllis Theroux, "Amazing Grace," *Washington Post*, October 18, 1981, www.washingtonpost.com/archive/lifestyle/magazine/1981/10/18 /amazing-grace/80c3d328-1270-4f50-90d8-ba72dc903b90/.

1 LEADERSHIP CHANGES THE WORLD: JOINING THE REVOLUTION

15   *Word for reconciliation is* katallagē: "2 Corinthians 5:19 Translation and Meaning," *Quotes Cosmos*, www.quotescosmos.com/bible/bible-verses/2-Corinthians-5-19 .html.

   Merriam-Webster defines reconcile: Merriam-Webster, s.v. "reconcile," www .merriam-webster.com/dictionary/reconcile.

17   *Our task as image-bearing*: N. T. Wright, *The Challenge of Jesus: Rediscovering Who Jesus Was and Is* (Downers Grove, IL: InterVarsity Press, 2015), 184.

3 SURRENDER: NOT MY WILL BUT THY WILL

34   *If you have only come*: Oswald Chambers, *My Utmost for His Highest* (Grand Rapids, MI: Discovery House, 1992).

37   *Why did God make you?*: Roman Catholic Church, *Baltimore Catechism* (New York: Benziger Brothers, 1933; repr., Charlotte, NC: TAN Books, 2010).

4 SACRIFICE: CAREER SUICIDE

44   *Definitions for the word* sacrifice: Merriam-Webster, s.v. "sacrifice," www.merriam -webster.com/dictionary/sacrifice.

6 EXCELLENCE: IT'S HOW YOU PLAY THE GAME

62   *Wells Fargo phony account scandal*: "Wells Fargo Phony Account Scandal, Explained," *The Week*, September 17, 2016, https://theweek.com/articles/649015 /wells-fargos-phonyaccount-scandal-explained.

66   *If we want to reignite innovation*: Brené Brown, *Daring Greatly: How the Courage to Be Vulnerable Transforms the Way We Live, Love, Parent, and Lead* (New York: Avery, 2012), 15.

   Of course we want to win: Attributed to Pete Carroll, www.azquotes.com /author/44751-Pete_Carroll.

66   *Two trips to the Super Bowl*: Andy Patton, "Pete Carroll Earns 100th Win as Seattle Seahawks Head Coach," *USA Today*, December 16, 2019, https://seahawkswire .usatoday.com/2019/12/16/pete-carroll-earns-100th-win-as-seattle-seahawks -head-coach/.

8 HUMILITY: THE EXECUTIVE TOILET

85   *True humility*: Rick Warren, *The Purpose Driven Life: What on Earth Am I Here For?* (Grand Rapids, MI: Zondervan, 2003).

10 VISION: SEEING A BETTER TOMORROW

107   *Brutal facts of reality*: Jim Collins, *Good to Great: Why Some Companies Make the Leap and Others Don't* (New York: HarperCollins, 2001), 69.

SWOT analysis: Mike Morrison, "SWOT Analysis (TOWS Matrix) Made Simple," *RapidBI*, April 20, 2016, https://rapidbi.com/SWOTanalysis/#Background.

11 COURAGE: DO NOT BE AFRAID

120   *Courage is not living without fear*: Attributed to Chae Richardson, https://juicy quotes.com/tag/chae-richardson/.

Courage is contagious: Billy Graham, "A Time for Moral Courage," *Reader's Digest*, July 1964.

122   *Just 3 percent*: Barna Group, "Omnipoll," 2002.

12 GENEROSITY (GREEDLESSNESS): THE TOXICITY OF MONEY

133   *Apple's goal*: Michael Cramton, "24 Quotes from the Genius Behind Apple," *Huffington Post*, August 25, 2011, www.huffpost.com/entry/25-quotes-from-the -genius_b_936437.

Opioid-based medications: Andrew Kolodny, "The Magnitude of America's Opioid Epidemic, in Six Charts," *Quartz*, November 6, 2017, https://qz.com/1112727/the -magnitude-of-americas-opioid-epidemic-in-six-charts/.

136   *2,350 verses about money*: Brandon Park, "2,350 Bible Verses on Money," *Church Leaders*, November 30, 2017, https://churchleaders.com/outreach-missions /outreach-missions-articles/314227-2350-bible-verses-money.html.

One out of every seven verses: "Money and Motives," Crosswalk.com, September 4, 2008, www.crosswalk.com/faith/spiritual-life/money-and-motives-11581312.html.

13 FORGIVENESS: I'M SORRY

151   *I want to begin by offering*: Transcript published in Justin Bariso, "With a New Apology, Starbucks's CEO Just Taught an Important Lesson in Leadership," *Inc*, April 16, 2018, www.inc.com/justin-bariso/after-arrest-incident-goes-viral-starbucks -ceo-kevin-johnson-issues-new-apology.html.

151 *Any person who enters*: Emily Stuart, "Starbucks Says Everyone's a Customer After Philadelphia Bias Incident," *Vox*, May 19, 2018, www.vox.com/identities/2018/5/19/17372164/starbucks-incident-bias-bathroom-policy-philadelphia.

Racial-bias training: Anna Orso, "One Year Later: A Timeline of Controversy and Progress Since the Starbucks Arrests Seen 'Round the World," *Philadelphia Inquirer*, April 12, 2019, www.inquirer.com/news/starbucks-incident-philadelphia-racial-bias-one-year-anniversary-stutter-dilworth-park-homeless-tables-20190412.html.

14 SELF-AWARENESS: KNOW THYSELF

160 *Wharton MBA class of 2021*: Kelly Vo, "Inside the Wharton MBA Class of 2021," *Clear Admit*, August 22, 2019, www.clearadmit.com/2019/08/inside-the-wharton-mba-class-of-2021-profile/.

15 BALANCE: ALL WORK AND NO PLAY

168 *Four hours of unpaid work*: Organization for Economic Cooperation and Development, "Employment: Time Spent in Paid and Unpaid Work, by Sex," https://stats.oecd.org/index.aspx?queryid=54757.

172 *Nobody on his deathbed*: Attributed to Paul Tsongas, https://en.wikiquote.org/wiki/Paul_Tsongas.

176 *Not all readers are leaders*: Attributed to Harry Truman in Christopher Pierznik, "20 Quotes About Books and Reading from Entrepreneurs and World Leaders," *Medium*, January 26, 2018, https://medium.com/the-passion-of-christopher-pierznik-books-rhymes/20-quotes-about-books-and-reading-from-entrepreneurs-and-world-leaders-8188a5519856.

Buffett spends five to six hours: Michael Simmons, "Bill Gates, Warren Buffett, and Oprah All Use the 5-Hour Rule," *Medium*, July 22, 2016, https://medium.com/accelerated-intelligence/bill-gates-warren-buffett-and-oprah-all-use-the-5-hour-rule-308f528b6363.

16 HUMOR: IF WE DON'T LAUGH, WE'LL CRY

181 *Always laugh when you can*: Attributed to Lord Byron in "120 Inspirational Quotes About Laughter," Laughter Online University, www.laughteronlineuniversity.com/quotes-about-laughter/.

Medical studies have shown: Maud Purcell, "The Healing Power of Humor," *Psych Central*, January 14, 2020, https://psychcentral.com/lib/the-healing-power-of-humor/.

182 *Laughter is the shortest distance*: Attributed to Victor Borge, www.goodreads.com/quotes/172-laughter-is-the-shortest-distance-between-two-people.

187 *If I am not allowed to laugh*: Attributed to Martin Luther in "The Best Quotes About Laughter," *Ranker*, June 14, 2019, www.ranker.com/list/notable-and -famous-laughter-quotes/reference.

17 ENCOURAGEMENT: WELL DONE, GOOD AND FAITHFUL SERVANT

194 *Treat a man as he is*: Stephen R. Covey, *The 7 Habits of Highly Effective People: Powerful Lessons in Personal Change* (New York: Simon & Schuster, 1989).

197 *Just a spoonful of sugar*: Richard M. Sherman and Robert B. Sherman, "A Spoonful of Sugar," *Mary Poppins (Original Soundtrack)*, Walt Disney Records, 1964.

18 PERSEVERANCE: HANG IN THERE

204 *It ain't about how hard*: *Rocky Balboa*, directed by Sylvester Stallone (Culver City, CA: Metro-Goldwyn-Mayer, 2006).

19 LISTENING: BEES DO IT

218 *Tell them about the dream*: Drew Hansen, "Mahalia Jackson, and King's Improvisation," *New York Times*, August 27, 2013, www.nytimes.com/2013/08/28 /opinion/mahalia-jackson-and-kings-rhetorical-improvisation.html?_r=0.

King's leadership style: John Blake, "The One Thing About Martin Luther King Jr.'s Greatness Everyone Keeps Missing," CNN, January 20, 2020, www.cnn .com/2020/01/20/us/martin-luther-king-jr-listener-blake/index.html.

219 *You have never talked*: Quoted in Roger Edwards, "Never Talked to a Mere Mortal," The Barnabas Center, September 3, 2013, http://thebarnabascenter.org /never-talked-to-a-mere-mortal/.

223 *The powerful truth*: James Surowiecki, *The Wisdom of Crowds* (New York: Doubleday, 2004), xi-xiii.

20 TAKING GOD TO WORK

233 *Why did God make you?*: Roman Catholic Church, *Baltimore Catechism* (New York: Benziger Brothers, 1933; repr., Charlotte, NC: TAN Books, 2010).

239 *I want Indian nuns*: David Scott, *A Revolution of Love: The Meaning of Mother Teresa* (Chicago: Loyola Press, 2005), 76.

I'm a little pencil: Attributed to Mother Teresa, www.goodreads.com /quotes/30608-i-m-a-little-pencil-in-the-hand-of-a-writing.

ALSO AVAILABLE

RICHARD STEARNS

LEAD
LIKE IT
MATTERS
TO
GOD

STUDY GUIDE

EIGHT SESSIONS **ON BECOMING
A VALUES-DRIVEN LEADER**